Always Left Smiling

Even in Darkness, She Counted Stars

JENNIFER BERNAY

Always Left Smiling

Even in Darkness, She Counted Stars

JENNIFER BERNAY

Printed and Electronic Versions
ISBN Book: 978-1-956353-81-5
ISBN eBook: 978-1-956353-82-2
(Jennifer Bernay / Motivation Champs)

The book was printed
in the United States of America.

To order additional copies or bulk order contact the publisher,
Motivation Champs Publishing.
www.motivationchamps.com

CONTENTS

PROLOGUE

One of my earliest memories takes place in the backyard of our first house on a sunny, warm day. My "five-year-old" self is standing in the neatly mowed grass, watching my dad throw a ball up into the bright blue sky. The heavens seem to swallow the target and then gently release it back to earth, much to my delight and those of my brothers. My senses are alive with the sweet smells and sights of summer: fresh-cut grass, the warmth of the sun on my skin, my thirst quenched with a grape popsicle, and hearing my brothers' voices squeal, "Do it again!" I could watch this for hours, as I am awe-stricken and fascinated by the sheer concept of how my dad seems to play catch with the heavens above my small body.

Ingrained in my mind is the joy in these and other moments, laughter and love filling our lives. My brothers, ages three and seven, and I are still learning to share and mind our manners. Our parents are young and busy, keeping us content and pursuing their dream of raising a family. My memories from childhood, at the age of five, are vivid but randomly sporadic. I remember crawling into the back seat of the baby blue '69 Ford Mustang convertible, amidst the baseball bats and baseballs, the dust from the baseball field filling my nose. The car was a gift my dad had purchased for my mom with the salary from his baseball days playing in the Boston Red Sox farm system. His "Sox" signing contract and payroll from those days (not much in today's leagues) were meager but allowed him to supplement his current teaching contract. After years of baseball and travel, he decided to walk away from his baseball career to marry my mom and raise a family.

Recalling my childhood, my days consisted of playing with neighborhood friends and attempting, but not always succeeding, to play with my brothers. Our house was busy with excitement, filled with the gatherings of cousins, aunts, uncles, and grandparents. To say it was idyllic and picturesque for a child was accurate; we had loving parents, food on the table, and a wonderful house. My mom filled the house with laughter, oftentimes as a result of my dad and his sense of humor. My mom, if I had to choose, seemed to be the stricter of the two, with my dad offering more "compassion" when settling arguments between my brothers and me. During a planned trip to Hershey World, for example, my brothers and I were loaded into the old brown station wagon while my parents completed loading the car. My older brother began arguing with me and settled the argument with a hit to my head. Of course, I reacted with tears and screaming, and my mom stated that we would have to cancel the trip altogether because we could not get along. Due to this altercation in the car, we were quickly escorted into the kitchen to discuss the situation. I sat on my dad's lap and calmed myself, more upset with the trip being canceled than the initial hit from my brother. As my mom moved around the kitchen, cleaning up dishes, my dad offered the suggestion that maybe we should still attempt the trip if my brother and I agreed to get along. My brother and I rejoiced in this suggestion, excitedly agreeing. I remember seeing the glare from my mom at him, as if she could not believe his graciousness in the moment and his seeming lack of awareness that she was teaching us a lesson: that we could lose privileges when we fought with each other.

They were a team with their parenting styles; my mom's stricter approach would often succumb to reasoning with my dad, resulting in a united front, as the lesson remained intact while satisfying the urge to create enjoyable moments. The memories I have of the time spent with the two of them are of watching them enjoy their lives, often with my mom erupting in her distinct laughter and my dad's smile that lit up the room. Unwittingly, he commanded the room with his confidence; his laid-back approach to situations often attracted conversations from those in his presence. He was approachable and engaging, and loved sharing his knowledge of baseball and sports. He was charismatic, and to me, he hung the moon. Together, they made our lives idyllic, and reflecting on this upbringing, I could not be more grateful.

They could always find humor in situations, as I am sure this instance was discussed "behind closed doors" after the fact, but the truth was that they were a united front in providing us with lessons, encouragement, and happy moments. Years later, watching home movies, I see them playfully posing for the camera; my parents' laughter is silent in the old films, but the happiness of the moments is captured in the antics. One clip shows my dad standing in our backyard, waving his arms and dancing, carefree and embroiled in putting on a show for the lens. In yet another clip, my mom is attempting to get us into the car for an event, fashionably dressed with a skirt and blouse. My dad is behind the movie camera, capturing the moment. She turns towards the camera, laughing and pretending to "hike up her skirt," flirting with the cameraman, and quickly adjusts herself not to expose too much leg, as I am sure they knew this would become a memory to show later in life. I remember hearing the sounds of their laughter, reflected in the innocence of their young lives.

My parents married young, in their early twenties, and both were educators. Dad chose to be a high school teacher and basketball coach, as he had played basketball and baseball in high school. Mom was drawn to teaching in early childhood, and, along with Dad, they settled into a beautiful life. They met in high school and were blissfully happy together, filling their home with children, family, friends, faith, and most of all laughter and love. Their future was promising, hopeful, and vast. They had planned many trips with us, birthday celebrations, and more.

God, however, had another plan for such a young, family man, just 34 years old.

The day began much like any Christmas in northeast Ohio in 1974. We jumped from our rooms to see what Santa had delivered. The hours that it took for Santa to wrap and bring presents, carefully fill the stockings, and steal away into the night were whittled down to the 30 minutes it would take for us to devour what Santa had left for us. With the newly fallen snow on the ground, it was cold outside, but the warmth of the house was alive with smells of Christmas morning, breakfast casserole, and the casseroles my mom was baking to take to our grandparents' house later that day. Each Christmas, after opening our gifts, we would settle into our day, packing up in the early afternoon to drive to my mom's parents' house for a celebration with our grandparents, aunts and uncles, and cousins. My grandparents hosted a dinner for all of us, and we would gather around a large table, sharing stories and enjoying dinner and Christmas cookies.

The next morning, I awoke to a house full of neighbors, family, and even strangers. I found my way through the tall grass of "legs" to our family room, to see my three-year-old brother and "recently-turned" eight-year-old brother playing with some of our new gifts, compliments of Santa. I remember the confusion of that morning. Why was our house full of people that morning? Where was Mom? Where was Dad? And why did everyone seem so sad? That was quickly answered when I saw Mom approach us, aided in walking by our uncle, my dad's brother, and our granddad, my mom's father. She approached hesitantly, her eyes swollen and her young, 33-year-old face pale and unrecognizable with sadness. Why was she unable to walk without help? Why did she look so tired and lost? After all, it was the day after Christmas, and my brothers and I were happily immersed in our new toys and gleefully getting along.

She slowly and quietly bent down to us as we played with the Fisher-Price workbench, hammering away at the colorful wooden nails and putting them in their corresponding holes.

She spoke softly and somewhat garbled in between catching her breath and bouts of crying. "Your Dad is not coming home anymore. He went to live in heaven with Candy" (referring to our puppy that had died after being hit by a car a year earlier). She seemed to have difficulty pronouncing the words as they left her mouth, yet the almost bluntness with which they flowed seemed forced, as if she were speaking but not truly believing what she was saying to us.

I honestly do not recall the next words that she spoke at that moment. Maybe it was from my five-year-old self not understanding the impact of her words, the finality of death, or shock, or both. She was then aided in rising to her feet and escorted from the room. Unable to process this profound, life-changing news, I remember being left with the feeling that Dad was on some sort of trip and would return one day soon. Reasoning that he would return, I went back to my workbench and attempted to entertain my younger brother. Interestingly enough, this is one of the vivid memories I have of that time, burned into my mind for reasons I would come to understand as an adult, and the enormity of this moment played a critical role in my life.

After this life-altering event, I recall another evocative memory of my mom escorting us to visit a beautiful, peaceful place. The grass was lush and green, with a small, private path in the road. It had a lake with ducks, and I remember spending a lot of time here, feeding the ducks and quietly contemplating why we were there. The significance of the peaceful solitude etched in my mind would eventually give way to my understanding of this place. It wasn't until a few years later that I would understand the importance of this place, the cemetery where my dad was laid to rest. We would drive there as if on autopilot, often in our brown station wagon, and I had not realized the impact of what it all meant to my mom. My dad had been hit by a car, a suspected drunk driver, in front of our house on Christmas night. He was helping a former student of his who had run out of gas, had siphoned some gas from our car, and was emptying it into the stranded vehicle when he was hit. Although unable to process this loss for myself at the time, it was years later, when I became a mother, that I was able to realize the courage and profound grace of my mom. The impact of this tragedy on her life, the end of her storybook "happily ever after," and now faced with raising a 3, 5, and 8-year-old alone.

CHAPTER ONE

Finding Courage

—

Courage was synonymous with my mom and shaped her approach to life in unimaginable ways. I never envisioned Mom could show us more courage than she did when Dad passed, but I was wrong. My mom, Nora, was born in Memphis, Tennessee, on March 17th, 1941. She was the middle child of two sisters, born into a life of contentment, nurtured by loving and supportive parents. They moved from Memphis and settled in Cuyahoga Falls, Ohio, when she was three years old. She endeared herself to many close friends during her high school journey, was homecoming queen, active in extracurricular activities, including cheerleading, and met her future husband, Harry, when she was sixteen. She went away to college, graduated with a BA in Elementary Education, and began her passion for teaching children.

Now, a young widow raising three children by herself, she was left to grapple with how to do this alone. I believe she was born with the innate ability to approach obstacles with courage, strength, and a resolve we would come to witness throughout her life. She struggled to find laughter but tried to bury herself in finding joy. She did not want us to see her in pain, how she would face each day alone. Years later, she confided in me that during those times after Dad passed, she would hide in the basement when she was doing laundry and bury her head in clothes to drown out the screams of anguish and tears of her loss. I imagine she could hear us running around upstairs, either arguing or jumping around the house, and with each sound, she was reminded of her situation. She said that she would call her mom, and using the signal they had worked out with the phone, my mom would let it ring once and then hang up. This "signal" would let my grandmother know she needed her. My mom told me that they used this signal because many times, she would not be able to even speak into the phone due to her pain.

My mom chose to sell our house a year after my dad passed, as she could not have the memories of the happiest time in her life coincide with the saddest time. Too many memories, the empty places in the house that he would fill, each corner of the house now painfully full of her loss. She sold the house, we moved into a neighborhood full of other children close to our ages, and she returned to work. She needed to find ways to support our family of four, pay for a house and a car, and save for future endeavors. During the day, she alternated between working as a bank teller and subbing in the local school districts. She also began taking classes in the evenings at a nearby college to renew her teaching license.

To many of us, this appears not only insurmountable and inconsolable, but I am sure she asked herself many times, "How did I get here?" And yet, she knew that she was needed to raise their children. She trusted her courage and faith and embraced her tragically altered path in life, although unable to fill that hole created that cold Christmas night.

My brothers and I were active in sports; each of us played baseball and softball in the local recreation leagues. She tried valiantly to attend each of our games, but with three children in sports, we learned to rely on carpools, and her attendance at some games was cut short due to her leaving to drive to watch another child's game. We participated in school functions, Cub Scouts, Brownies, music lessons, and did well academically. She was finally able to secure a job teaching elementary Title I students, a position she held until her retirement. She prepared dinner for us each night and would ask us to choose a vegetable and a fruit to accompany the meal. She also assigned chores to each of us, a way we could earn money and take some of the burden away from her, I can imagine. However, this organized task taught us responsibility and how to manage the money we earned as we got a little older. She helped us with homework, while creating her own lesson plans and grading, preparing dinners, keeping the house clean, organizing our finances, and finding time for us to enjoy our lives. We were her focus, and she was determined to do her best to make sure that we grew up happy and content.

Christmas mornings, tragically altered for her, were filled with joy for us, unable to grasp the enormity of the hollowness for her. She continued to work through the pain she endured, and Santa always made an appearance, fulfilling what gifts fit the budget, along with the desire to ensure Christmas mornings remained joyful for us. Never once did I imagine what strength she showcased in those Christmas morning rituals. She did tell me, as I got older, that she relied on the help of her parents on Christmas Eve, setting up toys, building dollhouses, and arranging the "loot." In fact, she recalled one toy she had chosen for my younger brother—a police car with lights and a siren that chirped when the batteries were in place. He really wanted the toy, as many young boys loved playing with toy police cars and trucks that made noise. She told me later how difficult it was for her to hear that toy in the house, the siren noise taking her back to that Christmas night. But he was thrilled with his gift, unbeknownst to him, as the simple sound of the siren and lights from the top of the toy car evoked the memory.

She took care of us, through many illnesses with compassion, and oftentimes, she relied on pure instinct to help us battle a cold, strep throat, or the flu. I recall one of many times, waking up in the night sick to my stomach and running to our bathroom to throw up, as many stomach bugs made their way through the house with younger children. She would always encourage us to drink Coke syrup to "calm our stomachs", as she would say. Only an hour later, we were back in the bathroom, sicker than before.

I am also reminded of a dinner she made once, as she was coordinating dinners with extracurricular after-school activities after a full day of work herself. She carefully prepared salmon patties, and we all commented on the smell of the final product. But she was proud of what she made, and my brothers and my mom went on to enjoy their dinner. I did not like seafood, so I chose not to eat that night. Hours later, they awoke, sick to their stomachs, running to the bathroom all night long from this endeavor, and I was so relieved that I had chosen not to eat the meal. Days later, we laughed at how sick they all were, and she promised not to make that again!

My brothers and I loved playing baseball and softball during the summer months in our local rec leagues. I reflect on this now and wonder if this appeal wasn't something inherited from our dad in some way, or from watching him throw the ball in our backyard, even though we never got to see him play professionally. Maybe it was the smell of the dust, and seeing baseballs and baseball bats, reminiscent of the blue Mustang, that fed our desire to play. But this desire to play sports was undeniable, and my mom enrolled us in the rec league each summer. I am sure she wondered how she could make it work with her work schedule and three young kids in sports. She organized schedules so that we could be placed on a team with someone she knew, to carpool to practices and games, as this feat could not be done alone. It became known to us that for some games, Mom would not be present or arrive late, and that was fine, as long as we were playing. My softball life soon became marred with injuries, broken fingers from the catcher position, and sprained wrists when I was moved to the second base position. In fact, during one of our trips to the hospital for X-rays, my mom was pulled aside and questioned by nurses! It was a revolving door for me: whether playing basketball or softball, riding my bike or roller-skating - the result usually involved a visit to the ER.

One summer day, Mom had to run to pick up a prescription at the pharmacy. She asked my older brother to be "in charge" while she ran to the pharmacy, as this would be a quick trip, and we were older; he was 15 and could babysit for a 30-minute errand. During this time, I told my brother that I was going to ride my bike around the block. Well, with my injury record, I inevitably fell from my bike and injured my wrist. The neighbor, whose house I was in front of at that time, came to my assistance and walked me home. My brother called the pharmacy to tell my mom (way before cell phones), and she rushed home. My brother had also called my dad's mom, our grandmother, and she rushed over, only to arrive before my mom. She told me how awful she felt about this, feeling that her mother-in-law probably wondered why she would leave us alone for this trip. I am sure my grandmother did not feel this way, but I can see why my mom felt this way at the time—another trip to the ER and more X-rays. But my mom put our needs ahead of her own and worked out ways to help us, albeit doing this alone; we never felt abandoned, wanting more, or not loved.

She also found time to bake banana bread and chocolate chip cookies, a favorite, which became a staple when she eventually had grandchildren! I remember helping her in the kitchen with baking and always finding time to laugh at ourselves. I remember baking chocolate chip cookies with her, and the two of us would eat the cookie dough or sandwich it between two baked cookies! I could watch her for hours in our kitchen, measuring the ingredients and using the hand mixer to combine them all into a wonderful, delicious concoction. Each time, she carefully ensured that I learned a trick, such as sifting the flour with the baking soda or chilling the dough before baking. She loved to share her knowledge and made sure I learned this tradition so I could pass it down to my own kids one day. Always the teacher!

The effort and organization she exuded in her "lessons" for us were inspiring and thoughtful, and she relied on this approach to her own life. After all, she was the breadwinner, caregiver, teacher, and confidant. She found time in this busy schedule to engage with friends on occasion and would host a bridge club at our house. She would work feverishly to make appetizers and desserts to serve and clean the house prior to these events. During these times, she would tell us not to eat the food and to make sure we did not leave a mess, as I can imagine the work preparing for this as an adult myself with children. I can attest to the fact that as I sit here writing this, she not only accomplished all of this but did so amazingly, leaving her beautiful impact on everyone around her.

My mom, as told to me by my grandmother (her mom), appeared to be the more dependent daughter, which concerned my grandmother when our dad passed. My mom relied heavily on her mom and her family to help her navigate life after that night. However, she was resilient in her approach to ensuring that my brothers and I would not only survive, but thrive. We planned trips each year to visit Lake Erie, renting a cottage at Gem Beach with my grandparents. This became tradition, and with each summer trip, I watched as my mom began to laugh and enjoy her blessings once again.

Lessons were taught during these trips, as I recall. We learned to embrace life by riding inner tubes in the waves, having family dinners on the porch, building castles in the sand,

and playing board games in the evenings. These moments might seem insignificant, but the joy, camaraderie, and warmth felt with each visit to the cottage extended well past those four walls. Our independence and sense of responsibility were infused with taking care of each other during those trips. We became stronger as a family of four, relying on each other for laughter, strengthening our bond, and learning to rely only on those we had with us. I remember my mom's repetitive response to my complaints about my brothers being mean to me. She said, "I always wanted brothers," which always made me cringe. How significant that statement would become as I got older, and how it would play such a critical role in mending my heart in the coming years.

CHAPTER TWO

Love Renewed

—

After twelve years of focusing on her children and navigating a life by herself, she met Gene, a principal at our high school, at one of my basketball games. He was a divorced father of three boys. The boys, roughly the same age as we were at the time, attended school in the neighboring district. After a year of dating, they were married, and he moved into the house, and together they formed a family with six teenagers. More brothers to share a home with, although they only came for visits on weekends since they split their time between their parents. The adjustment took some time, as we learned to open our hearts to someone to share in our mom's focus. Our once-small group of four became a table of eight!

High school graduations, college life, marriages, and grandchildren filled their lives. I remember planning my wedding. What a wonderful time that was, not only with my life and future husband, but also with the memories of planning this with my mom. Dave, my future husband, and I had reluctantly moved to Florida for jobs, and most of the planning had fallen to my mom, who seemed eager to coordinate the wedding. We were getting married in my hometown, and she arranged the florist selection and cake tasting, and together we shopped for a wedding dress. After the wedding, she helped arrange for our gifts to be sent to us in Florida—some shipped and some personally delivered by them during a future visit. They loved to travel, entertain friends and family, embrace their second act, and live for spending time with their children and grandchildren. My mom retired from teaching shortly after our first son was born, and she could not wait to spend more time with her grandchildren.

Another fond memory I have occurred when I was approaching my due date for our first son, prior to her retirement. Dave and I were living in Florida, and I talked endlessly on the phone with my mom trying to coordinate their arrival when he was born. We decided that they would have their bags packed and ready and wait for my phone call to say I was in labor. My mom planned to stay with us for the first month, and Gene would drive home after a week. However, many of us know that birth plans do not always end up the way we envision. So, I began contractions and placed the call. Gene picked my mom up from her classroom, and they began the 16-hour drive to Tampa. I panicked, thinking that they would never make it all the way down for the birth, but I was relieved to know they were on their way. Dave and I went to the hospital after my phone call and spent the next few hours waiting for the contractions to become more regular. This did not happen, and they sent us home to wait. I called Mom, somewhat disappointed in the lack of labor progression, and she told me that they had made it to Georgia and would stop for the night. Again, I thought they would not make it in time.

The next morning arrived with no progression, so Dave and I went about our day, our normal routine, prepping to make sure we had everything in place for our new arrival. At 5 PM, my water broke, and I knew that this trip to the hospital would result in us not leaving without a baby. I called my mom, and she said they were approaching Jacksonville and that they thought it would be a few more hours. I explained our situation and told them to meet us at the hospital, as we would be there for the duration. Our son arrived at 8:01 PM, and the first voice I heard from the other side of the door was my mom's laugh and her high-pitched voice saying something like "oh my gosh." I initially thought it was just my head playing tricks on me, the medication for the birth taking its toll on my senses, or my wishful thinking. But when Dave left the room with our son to take the normal baby measurements, he was greeted by my mom and Gene, who were excitedly awaiting the news! They had made it, just in time to meet our son minutes after he was born! God moments like this were inspiring, welcomed, and recognized - what a blessing in that moment and in the role they would play in years to come.

Our careers and the call of home took our young family back to Ohio. I never regretted this decision one bit. She truly loved being a Nana to her grandchildren. I recall her saying to me how much she loved hearing the word Nana; witnessing the joy of tiny feet and giggles, and feeling her heart expand with each addition. She loved watching our kids, to allow us a brief respite on a "date night" or a weekend away. She would greet us on each visit with a bag of teacher games, board games, chocolate chip cookies, and banana bread! Whether they would drive the two hours to our house or welcome us home, the routine was always the same, and the grandchildren loved every minute of it. I loved watching her interact with each of them, creating thoughtful conversations, filling their little lives with love and enjoyment, and focusing on their individuality. It provided a glimpse into how she must have interacted with us as children all those years ago. And all I could think was I hope I can be as good a mom and grandmother as she is. After each weekend together, we would all leave wanting more and looking forward to our next visit. We always left smiling.

I had always relied on her strength and at the age of fifty, began to believe more in myself and my passions thanks to her support and encouragement. So many times, I revert to that feeling of being blessed with a wonderful marriage, and together we were busy raising three healthy and beautiful children of our own, and a new master's degree that I had finally completed. Even as I type this, I am left with that feeling of the promise of things to come—celebrating milestones, and engaging with family and friends—what I wouldn't give to go back to that moment in time and live in it a little longer.

And then, when I thought I had finished witnessing her courage, grace, and faith, I was once again reminded of God's grace and that each day is a gift, not to be taken for granted, as every morning is never guaranteed.

Growing up, I began to use writing as a means of conveying my thoughts and feelings. It began when I entered my teenage years, when I started documenting my emotions in a diary, attempting to rationalize what I was going through. I continued to journal as I got older, and it brought me comfort, as if it eased my soul to express life's situations on paper. It was easier for me to write as opposed to engaging in conversation, as the words flowed more readily on paper than what I could convey with speaking. I found that this form of expression came in handy when writing for school and college, and slowly I began to use it when faced with a challenge, writing my thoughts down on paper prior to speaking with someone or as notes when addressing groups of people. I could reread and analyze why I documented certain notes and apply some reasoning to help me. This cathartic approach for me was working until I was faced with a life-changing situation, and, as much as I tried, I could not analyze or determine how to cope.

In 2020, the world experienced a pandemic that I had not faced in my lifetime. People were told to isolate themselves, so you can imagine the subject of that initial journal! My journals quickly shifted into letters that were specifically targeted to my mom, documenting what she was going through and referencing my diligent note-taking. I collected all the letters I had written to her and started reading them again and again. The memories transported me back to the time of attempting to work through my feelings and emotions, rationalizing my sense of purpose and determination, and trying to work through each frightening and heartbreaking moment as it came. Even now, it's difficult to read these letters because of the crushing awareness of why they stopped abruptly and the helplessness of knowing my inability to change the outcome.

Mom was diagnosed with Amyotrophic Lateral Sclerosis (ALS), or Lou Gehrig's Disease, at the age of 79. Reflecting back to that time, I wonder now if her symptoms hadn't begun earlier; regardless, we were somehow blissfully unaware of the trajectory of this cruel disease until her diagnosis. I was asked several times during my research into the disease whether my mom had been an athlete, possibly a runner, as the disease can disproportionately target these groups. The question seemed absurd to me; although she had been a high school cheerleader—and in fact could do splits well into her 70s—my mom did not even like to sweat. Her athleticism was confined to playing yard games with her children and grandchildren and dancing at weddings. She was not a veteran, male, nor did the disease run in her family, two other potential indicators. She never once complained about the diagnosis or became bitter with the news. In fact, she chose to live in each moment and prepared to enter this battle with positivity, reflection on her blessings, and the assurance that each of us would know she would not give up on her fight. She expressed her love for each of us and gracefully turned her hopeless diagnosis into powerful lessons in coming to terms with the inevitable outcome of ALS. That, in itself, is one of the life lessons that I will keep with me when facing insurmountable obstacles.

Prefacing my journal with some background knowledge of my mom might better explain her family's initial denial of her diagnosis; an illness such as ALS just did not "fit" with who my mom was. Now an unwitting and knowledgeable fundraiser and advocate for those waging the same battle as my mom once did, I am continually alarmed and terrified by the statistics surrounding ALS. This disease can strike anyone at any time, averaging approximately 5,000 new cases a year (according to the ALS Association statistics). Yet, there remains a long way to go to provide anything like a cure or even answers to the questions of those living with ALS, or to those left behind by those who have died. ALS was first identified in 1869 and was brought to the attention of many when baseball legend Lou Gehrig was given the devastating news of his diagnosis in 1939. How has this existed for so many years, with still no offer of hope for its cure or even an effective treatment? Although my mom was diagnosed in her late 70s, she was otherwise healthy and very active, traveling the country and engaging with friends and family. She had a lot left to do, more lives to impact, more love to share, more logic to impart. She was not done, despite her age, not by a long shot.

One image that still stands out to me and that I imagine for all of those who watch the rapid decline of loved ones, is how the professionals who treated and cared for her saw a woman who was silent, frail, and physically weak, descriptions that up until her diagnosis were antithetical to who my mom actually was. They had no idea who she was prior to the disease that, to them at least, now defined her. They could not see the history, the vast experiences, the deep and well-earned insight of the woman sitting in the chair in front of them, who no longer had the ability to talk. For my mom's entire life, her boundless empathy and contagious laughter enveloped all who were in her presence; strangers were only friends that she hadn't met. Her laugh could fill the room, and her smile could bring light to the darkest of places. She had the kind of inner strength that could change the life of another just by knowing her. That was not evident to those who cared for her during the last months of her life. My hope in sharing these letters is to provide a glimpse into who she was, into how she approached her battle with ALS, and her unrelenting power of love and refusal to ever stop counting her blessings. It is also my hope that by sharing her story, one person might discover a suggestion or an answer to an unresolved symptom that they have been investigating. Or possibly, one could learn about the power of resilience and how this can transform the spirit when faced with a terminal diagnosis.

CHAPTER THREE

First Signs

—

It started with her foot, that damn "foot drop", a term I dismissed as something that would go away with therapy. After all, she was healthy, active, and engaged with life. She explained that she had noticed this "foot drop" after a flight traveling to New Mexico to see friends. She was in her mid-70s, and we attributed it to the flight and even commented that maybe compression socks would have helped her. She had also been fighting edema in her legs, along with occasional leg cramps/ spasms. We believed that upon her return, she could see her doctor to investigate possible causes of her "foot drop," as she was becoming concerned and did not want to risk falling if her foot gave way while walking. She even chose to "err on the side of caution" and get herself a walking stick! She was not experiencing any pain in her foot, and the occasional flop of her foot, as if it just stopped working at times, was her main concern.

The "foot drop" (as we were told) was somewhat of a dilemma. Why was this happening, and how could she fix it? Thus began her search for answers. During that initial year of investigating, she encountered falls, broken bones, and numerous tests. Thinking back to January 2020, I was looking forward to the upcoming year, full of new beginnings, birthday celebrations, and celebrating high school graduation for our oldest. Mom was struggling with her unexplained symptoms, the previously-mentioned foot drop, occasional leg cramps, losing her "pucker" every once in a while, and experiencing accidental falls. She visited multiple doctors during her quest to find answers for her symptoms. She visited her PCP (primary care physician) on several occasions, once due to her swollen ankles and feet, asking what was causing this edema. She was told that it was a condition that affects older people, and she was prescribed some water pills to help with fluid retention. No tests were ordered, and once again, a missed opportunity to investigate her symptoms.

Early in 2020, she saw a spinal doctor based on a referral from a friend who had spinal/back issues, and the friend thought that this may be the culprit of her symptoms. This doctor explained to her that she had a compressed nerve in her spine. The doctor believed that her "foot drop" was attributed to this compressed nerve, along with her untreated scoliosis. Finally, a possible answer to her problem! This answer explained some of her symptoms, but strangely, not all of them. However, she reluctantly but eagerly scheduled spinal surgery to "get her life back." We were hopeful, but hesitant, as we awaited her surgery date. It was scheduled for late March of 2020.

But as March 2020 arrived, the world was introduced to the COVID-19 pandemic. Due to the pandemic, her surgery was postponed until late May of that year, and her courageous battle began. We communicated daily on the phone and used our Echo Show to see her. I remember calling her on the Echo Show to share the news that our oldest child had been accepted into the college of his choice; her enthusiasm was so contagious it jumped off the screen! However, she had other thoughts on her mind as her surgery date approached. Only this surgery was different due to the restrictions in place due to the pandemic. She would be going into the hospital, a "hot zone" of the pandemic, alone.

I can't imagine what she must have been thinking, terrified and anxious about making it through the spinal surgery, or terrified and anxious that she wouldn't. Either way, she bravely scheduled the surgery, knowing that she would have to do this without any family present for the surgery prep, recovery, and ultimate rehab. But her bravery, in the face of every obstacle, was now emerging. Although we had seen this displayed her entire life, now others were beginning to see it.

One day, while on the phone with her prior to her surgery, we discussed our oldest son's upcoming graduation from high school. Due to the pandemic, he would not walk across a stage in an auditorium full of students and families; instead, he would walk across the high school football field alone to receive his diploma. Not the type of graduation we all imagined, but we had all of the pride that encompasses this rite of passage. We talked about having her see all of us before her surgery, and we decided to drive halfway to meet each other and talk through the open car windows. Although not ideal, at least we could see each other's faces in person! A few hours before my family was due to leave to meet them halfway, she called and told me that she had to cancel our meeting, as she could not fathom if she had to use the restroom, move, or stretch her legs, she could do so easily with her current situation. She was heartbroken and cried on the phone at this missed opportunity. I knew the importance of seeing her, as my heart needed this interaction, if only through a window. We quickly decided that we, my husband, children, and our dog, would make the full trip, complete with a basket of goodies that she could enjoy during her upcoming hospital stay. We asked our oldest son to bring his cap and gown with him so that she could see him celebrate his milestone, to which he enthusiastically complied!

We arrived with our kids and dog and ventured around the outside of the house to meet her on their deck. It was a beautiful, sunny day, with the sun peaking through the young leaves on the trees. It was nice to feel the warmth from the sun and be outside. A neighbor's dog barked in the distance, and the familiar sounds of voices filled the yard, eagerly sharing what we had been doing during our isolation at home. While we stood outside, and she sat on their screened-in porch, we played the graduation song, "Pomp and Circumstance," on our phones while our son walked around from the side yard in his cap and gown. She was giddy with delight as she saw him approach the screen door, and she cried at the sight of him. As he met us, she was overcome with emotion and pride at witnessing his achievement. We talked through the screened door and briefly touched hands through the screen, careful to use Purell on our hands after our encounter. It was so good to see her in person, and I could not get enough of our conversation, even after spending hours on the phone daily with her. I could not hug her or console her, and it broke my heart, but being able to see her and hear her voice in person was therapeutic for my soul. She looked at the poster board full of pictures from our son's younger days, meant for a graduation party that would never happen, but the memories of those times were palpable in the moment. We presented her with a separate poster board, full of good-luck wishes that we wrote so she could display it in her hospital room as a reminder of her strength and perseverance, which would be welcome during her recovery over the next few weeks.

My mind races back to that time, imagining how scared she must have been, but I had seen her resilience my whole life, and I knew if anyone could do this, she could. And she did, although not easily. I remember calling her during her hospital stay, trying to reach her to hear her voice on the other end of the phone—my only means of knowing that she was still with us. We had to rely on the nurses to make sure that the phone was within reach of her hospital bed, as she could not move to answer my calls. I remember my first phone call to her room after speaking with the nurse's station, where I was reassured that she was settled in and awake to talk. I called the room, but it remained unanswered after several rings. I then realized that her phone must not be accessible to her, as they had mentioned. My heart began to ache as I determined that she could hear it ringing, but she was unable to reach the phone in the room without someone bringing it closer to her. How that must have felt for her, wanting to talk to loved ones but requiring assistance to make this happen. One of many times that, ironically, would dictate our future connections to her, relying on others to aid in our desire to communicate. They finally moved the phone closer to her after calling the nurse's station inquiring about this. During this time, I remember speaking with her on the phone and hearing her concern when she would "run out of breath," as she put it. We attributed it to the fact that she had just had major surgery, and she was on medications for pain.

God, how I wish now that this was the reason.

CHAPTER FOUR

Strength Stirred

—

Completely isolated and alone, she endured the surgery and subsequent rehab and returned home in late June. She arrived home and continued building her strength. Her breathing was still a concern, as she would become tired easily and had some difficulty walking with the walker. She had a follow-up appointment with her back surgeon, and he discovered after listening to her symptoms and running tests that she had blood clots in each leg and a pulmonary embolism in her lung. Terrifying at the time, but this provided some answers as to her fatigue, and in my mind, perhaps some resolution to her difficulty "catching her breath." She was put on medications to address her condition. Now she could focus on becoming stronger and getting her life back on track.

Together, she and Gene had made the decision to install a stair lift in their home months earlier, so she could manage the steps upstairs to their bedroom. When her "drop foot" had become an increasing concern, she and Gene, who had been married for 34 years at the time, had chosen to address the situation with a stair lift. How incredibly helpful that device became in her recovery at home. I was finally able to schedule a time to visit with her! I vividly remember the day I visited her at home in early July. One of my many lingering memories of this time was seeing her beautiful face through my mask. We stood (with her using her walker for support) in the kitchen, and I gave her a long, endearing hug. I felt the tears streaming down my face as I stood there sobbing, finally able to see her and so relieved that she had made it through surgery and rehab. I recall wondering why my tears took me by surprise. I attributed it to the fact that the sheer enormity of the surgery and the thought of her not surviving it was all encompassed in that long kitchen hug. I am so glad that I thoroughly lived in that moment, as it was the last hug from her when we both stood to greet each other. I now only wish I had hugged her longer. She was working on moving from room to room with her walker, paying close attention to her movements as she navigated the wooden ramps installed for the step-down family room and screened-in porch. She had recently graduated from the in-home OT and PT, and proudly demonstrated her seemingly improved drop foot. Still, I also noticed that she wasn't contributing to the conversation as much as she normally did, something I brushed off as she settled into a return to normal and recovery from her intense back surgery and subsequent rehab. We had dinner, and I recall she wasn't eating very much; she was just happily glancing around the porch, cherishing being with her family. I didn't think twice about her lack of appetite that day, but it was something I noticed. Then came August 11th, the evening of her accidental fall at home after attempting to head to bed using her walker to navigate the wooden ramp independently, resulting in a broken leg. This incident would become the pivotal turning point in all of our lives.

Another trip to the hospital, and more time I would not see her in person. So much of her battle was done alone. She was discharged to a rehab facility at a nursing home, one of the many heartbreaking decisions made at that time. Specifically because visitors were not allowed due to the pandemic, and, in addition, nursing homes were another "hot spot" for COVID-19 outbreaks. She requested to be moved to a nursing home rehab facility, as she believed providing care for her at home would be insurmountable due to her limitations of being non-weight bearing while her leg healed. During this time, I was unable to hug her or feel her hand in mine. We relied on a glimpse of her through a window and touching her hand through the screen. We began attempting conversations through a mask at the window, but slowly, I began to notice her voice and breathing diminish during our daily phone calls. Bravery came through in its truest form as she exemplified a grace and resilience that many of us cannot fathom. I soon found my new purpose, that her fight was now my fight. We focused on what she can do (and less on what she couldn't), and she lovingly entertained that thought, albeit voiceless, wheelchair-bound, and dependent on others. The only way to convey my support was to begin writing these letters to her, offering encouragement, love, and most of all, pride in having her as my mom.

I began documenting my feelings through journaling and letters to her. My mom read all of these letters, even the ones that I wrote to help me process. My first thoughts were documented in September 2020 after I made the drive to visit her at the window of the nursing home. I initially wrote these letters with the sole purpose of expressing my feelings at the time. I envisioned giving the first letter to my mom after she recovered from her nursing home stay, as soon as she returned home. I could almost see reading it to her in person or over the phone and listening to her response. These letters quickly turned into pages and pages of soul searching, anguish, and documenting a process of coping while honoring my mom and her spirit. After reading the first letter to her, I could hear the breathiness in her voice, and she said that the letter was beautiful and brought her to tears, which was difficult due to her condition. Due to this, I saved some of these letters, which were dedicated to my mom, and presented them to her on her 80th birthday for her to read when she could. I gave her the "I Can" poem for Christmas, in hopes of inspiring her. Between her initial diagnosis and her

80th birthday, there were 138 days - not enough time to process, research, and advocate, and provide her with other joys to focus on, and not what I was grappling with in my mind. Many of the letters had to wait for delivery to her, as there was too much to process at once.

September 21, 2020

As I look over at our sixteen-year-old second-born sleeping, the sunlight streaming through the windows of the car, I reflect on our situation. We are making the drive up north to visit my mom at the window of her nursing facility, which has restricted visitors due to the pandemic. It is during this drive that I begin to realize the importance of the cycle of our lives.

I travel back to a time when I was younger, searching for answers, advice, and strength from my mom. She is my "rock" of inspiration, the foundation of our family. Her life is remarkable, accented by laughter, heartbreak, triumphs, and love. But what resonates with me the most is her undeniable determination to make the best of life's ups and downs, all with her keen sense of humor, perseverance, and strength. She is the strongest woman I know.

She has supported me through life's moments, good and bad, and shown me how to handle diversity with grace and humor. When I had children of my own, I learned so much from her, watching her interact, play, and relish in the innocence of my children. She lived for moments when they could watch the kids so we could enjoy a night out, got up early to allow us extra sleep, read books, and lovingly put the kids to bed during our visits.

And now it is our turn. It amazes me that now my kids lovingly take care of her, helping her move to another room, holding her arm as she balances while walking, and encouraging her as she battles her aging body. The life cycle is truly amazing, and heartbreaking at the same time. But I now understand the process, for everything she has done for me has brought me to this moment, taking care of my mom. Her fragility is apparent, and I can now see that she is fallible, which makes this all the more difficult. However, the determination and strength she has exhibited her whole life are on full display, making me even more proud to call her mom.

As we finish the drive in the car, I realize that we've come full circle and it is our turn to watch them, allowing them to sleep peacefully when they need it, and reading books and lovingly helping them to bed. And now I understand that all of these acts are done so with an overwhelming abundance of love. This cycle has taught me strength, wisdom, advocacy, and an undeniable love of life. Keep on fighting, Mom. You're amazing, cherished, and still my rock and inspiration.

CHAPTER FIVE

Looking for Hope

———

During the time of her nursing home rehab, late September and early October 2020, our phone conversations, my only means of communicating with her, began to hasten due to her "running out of breath." She would begin the conversation with, "Hello, my darling daughter," and tell me about her recent experiences at the facility, and how she had noticed her speech was beginning to slur. In fact, her comment at the time was that she said she sounded "drunk" every once in a while. She was also noticing difficulty eating the foods they provided, as chewing and swallowing needed more of her focus. Her stories of her care there made my heart ache, though she would always make sure the care sounded better than I knew it was. There were aides not wearing masks, and she did not want to repeatedly remind them, in case they would not want to help her if she sounded demanding. She needed assistance getting up and using the bathroom, often pressing her call light button only to sit there waiting for 45 minutes for a response. On several occasions, help would arrive too late. She would be subjected to lying in her soiled bed, dependent on strangers to assist her. She tried to reason with the aides in an empathetic manner, stating that she didn't want to bother them as she knew how busy they were taking care of others, but at the same time, she would, unfortunately, need assistance with simple tasks that she could do on her own up until now. This pleading, however, did not change the outcome of her care, as we noticed that this became a daily routine, waiting too long to get help after pressing her button, food that she could not consume due to her ever-changing swallowing difficulties, and sometimes choking on her water. My phone calls to the nurse's station and nursing home management only made her care seem worse, so she asked me not to mention it anymore, and she would cope with what she was given.

I began asking what she had done each day, and we began focusing on what she "could do" rather than what she "couldn't do." During these calls, she would describe how she was still experiencing trouble catching and keeping her breath, often running out of breath while trying to muster enough to continue the conversation. I reasoned with myself that this was a result of not getting adequate care and therapy to build her strength, combined with her lack of movement. Out of concern, I placed phone calls to the aide's station multiple times due to her breathing, afraid that she would choke or could not catch her breath. Could this be an asthmatic attack? Did she contract pneumonia or COVID-19? But in reality, I was beginning to realize that something was terribly wrong, although I was not yet ready to admit it. I remember she ended one of our phone conversations with a winded "I love everything about you," to which I replied, I love everything about you, too! Our phone calls became my avenue to ensure she was still fighting to come home, which was never in doubt; however, I knew she was starting to wonder about her future independence. How would she navigate coming home to a two-story house and a step-down family room, where she fell in August?

She empathetically chose to move into an independent living apartment, across the grounds from the nursing facility, so as not to burden Gene or us with her increasingly needed care. It was a completely furnished 2-bedroom apartment and had a small kitchen. One of the bedrooms had room for a hospital bed, which she would need during her recovery, and room to maneuver a wheelchair, which she would require until her leg finished healing. It seemed ideal, she would return to be with her family and recuperate, while providing reassurance that help could be there if needed, with the push of a button. I could hardly wait to see her again, her beautiful face, and hug her and hold her hand. On October 3, 2020, Dave and I met them at their apartment as they wheeled her over from the nursing home facility. Once again, overcome with emotions, I cried at the very sight of her in front of me, and I could see the excitement in her smile, but I noted a hint of apprehension as well. As tears welled in her eyes, she told me that she was having trouble catching her breath when she cried, so crying is not an option. I don't know if she was trying to calm my emotions by "selling it to me" or merely coming to terms with the fact that she knew something was wrong.

Gene and Dave carefully unpacked the kitchen items that were brought from our house, as my mom and I arranged her room and bed, all with the intention that this would be temporary. The room was a nice size, complete with a large closet and two windows that let in the bright sunlight. The view from the ground-floor window provided an ample glimpse of the leaves changing color, though one had to look past the parking lot directly outside to catch sight of the changing season. I eagerly helped her organize her clothes, putting the items she wanted in the drawers. The room held two dressers, along with an individual bathroom with a shower. The bathroom was equipped with grab bars, a "roll-in shower", and a sink and vanity. We peppered the windowsills with all of the get-well cards she had received, striving to make the room more cheerful and to provide inspiration. I recall that this layout would be sufficient until she could return to the house in a month.

After unpacking and getting them both settled, we went on a tour of the apartment grounds, marveling at the sights of the architecture and landscaping as we wheeled her around the cement walkway and discussed the flowers that accentuated the outside. There was also an indoor pool available for use by residents, and I remember commenting that it could help with mobility once she was feeling stronger. It was during this visit that I started to see how frail and weak she had become in the last month, struggling to talk, catching her breath, and not having the strength to go from the wheelchair to the Sara Stedy, a device used to get her to the bathroom. Using the Sara Stedy, we could lift her from her seated position, using a gait belt for support, onto this device. Her only requirement was to use any strength she had left to assist us with this lift, focusing on her arm strength and grip, as she held her failing muscles in a standing position until we could lock in the seated pad behind her. Once she was positioned, we could rely on the wheels of this device to guide her across the floor to the restroom. Her body was seemingly not cooperating with her mind's requests to move. Her sense of humor and smile were intact, and while holding her hand, I could feel the strength of her grip, which was reassuring to my ever-growing concerns. As she held my hand in hers, her grip was as if she was squeezing so hard it was as if she never wanted to let it go. Ironically, neither did I, and we held hands for most of this visit. When we left for our home that day, I remember feeling ecstatic and relieved to finally see her in person, but concern for her was at the forefront of my mind.

A few days later, she was taken to see her pulmonologist, at our request, to investigate her breathlessness. She was sent immediately to the hospital for more testing, as the pulmonologist knew her condition was not pulmonary-related. Again, more testing at the hospital was needed, and more isolation from her family. During her stay, a nurse noticed that she choked while drinking water through a straw and proceeded only to allow her ice chips to quench her thirst, as they did not want her to aspirate. I remember her telling me how upset she was with this, as the ice chips were difficult to chew and did not seem to help her thirst. They had also begun to give her "thickened" coffee, another horribly-tasting option. But she, as always, complied with what she was told. She continued to work on building her strength through the physical therapy exercises she was given in her room and endured many more tests, including a modified barium swallow study (also known as a swallow test, or a "cookie test"), a CT scan, and blood tests. One possible diagnosis that arose was that she could have Myasthenia Gravis, a condition associated with muscle weakness. The doctor ordered a plasmapheresis treatment course to help get her strength back. It would be done in three grueling stages, and we were somewhat hopeful to receive a diagnosis that fit her symptoms and offered a solution.

After the first treatment, she was extremely tired and nauseous. The ice chips were of no help, and without her appetite, she was beginning to weaken. After the second treatment, it was determined that these transfusions were not helping her; in fact, they were making her increasingly weaker than before. It was then that my brothers and I received the call to come to the hospital, a call I dreaded more than anything. This, as it turned out, would be the first of many of those "dreaded phone calls" that we would experience in the coming months.

When we arrived, we were allowed to see her one at a time due to the ongoing pandemic concerns. Prior to heading to her room, we had a meeting with the doctor in a small sitting area of the hospital. My husband, Dave, Gene, my brother Bud, and I were present for the meeting. We used FaceTime to include our younger brother, Mike, from his home in North Carolina. The doctor was upfront and honest, and his demeanor was calm, confident, and empathetic. "Your Mom is weak and very sick," he began.

The tests show that it was not Myasthenia Gravis but a type of neurodegenerative disease. This did not make any sense to me, and I believe my brain immediately went into a type of "denial" mode. My mind raced with questions - what is a neurodegenerative disease? How did this happen? Did all of the testing/sitting/surgeries cause this? Fix her now! I asked what could be done to improve this, and his response still lingers with me today. He explained that there was nothing that could be done, and we needed to begin to think of options, as she was very sick. He wanted to refer her to a doctor in Cleveland who was a specialist for ALS, as her test results and symptoms pointed to a neurodegenerative disease. This statement was so far from what I could digest at this visit that I experienced an anger of sorts with this news. That can't be right. Mom is strong, vivacious, and independent; she can't be this sick or weak. She was the one who helped us get through our illnesses, trials, and life. How are we here?

Armed with this "denial," I made my way up to see her in her room. My mask covered my mouth and nose, and the shock of seeing her in that hospital bed took my breath away. I stepped into the room as she was sleeping, looking gaunt, weak, dehydrated, pale, and so much older. I gently woke her, and she greeted me with a weak smile. Her beautiful blue eyes danced with joy at the sight of me. I explained that they allowed us to visit as a surprise, but I often wonder if she knew why we were called to come.

She attempted to talk, but quickly resorted to writing to communicate, her eyes closing and nodding off to sleep. She summoned all her energy to write a note telling me how she did not want the third treatment, referring to the plasmapheresis. She was too weak and did not want to go through that again. I told the nurse and the doctor her request immediately after our encounter. I gently brushed her hair with my hands, and a smile swept across her sleeping face. I believe it reminded her, as it did me, of one of many memories from years ago that found its way into my mind. The memory centered on my younger self sleepily climbing into her bed in the morning and feeling her stroke my hair, a half-hearted attempt at waking me. Only this time, I was half-attempting to wake her from her slumber, wishing it was a bad dream and not reality. I solemnly left her room to allow Bud the opportunity to see her. We had promised to FaceTime with Mike so he could see her as well, so that became Bud's responsibility.

Riding the elevator back to the first floor, I fought the tears that had begun when I stepped from her room. Bud returned from his visit with her along with a note she had written: "Never been sicker. 3 nice surprises, so proud of my kids."

She was sent away again, to a hospital in Cleveland. It would be another three weeks before I would see her again, but I was hoping that they would discover how wrong this doctor was with his diagnosis. At the end of October, she was diagnosed with ALS. Again, I asked the doctor to rule out other diseases that mimic ALS, as she cannot have this terrible disease. After all, she has been healthy her whole life, and she is 79 years of age, and this disease doesn't run in our family. There has to be a mistake. Anything but ALS, as there is no cure, no hope. I called and arranged for a second opinion from a specialist: Lyme disease, Guillain-Barré syndrome, anything but ALS. Not only was this diagnosis confirmed, but this specialist noted that she was in the advanced stages of sporadic ALS. My denial took a backseat to my new, heartbreaking reality. This next letter was written to her after hearing this news.

October 25, 2020

I always thought we'd have more time. To hear your laugh, feel your hugs, and see your smile. Learn from your grace and heed your advice. The memories are endless: visiting Lake Erie, delighting in the inside jokes, asking advice about sewing, baking, and child-rearing. You always have a way of lightening the mood, looking for the lesson, and teaching during struggles.

I thought we'd have more time. To watch you interact with others, tell a story, bake chocolate chip cookies and banana bread, and engage with your grandchildren. I love watching you play a game with the kids while quietly ensuring they are doing well, elicit some memorable quotes, and just have fun with life.

I thought we'd have more time. To hear your voice, smell your perfume, and share funny anecdotes about our day- celebrate milestones, and count our blessings. You genuinely care about every soul you encounter and always make an impact. You once quipped that you "have big shoes to fill" when we lost our Nana, your Mom. If you only know how much you outgrew them.

I thought we'd have more time. To gather as a family, reminisce about our own childhood, create new traditions, and get together for birthdays and holidays. I recall once reading about a saying that said the important things in life are how you spend your dash, from birth to eternal life. That truly resonates with me as I look over your dash – filled with so many blessings, hardships, and triumphs. You are truly the best mom, wife, Nana, sister, Aunt, and friend.

I thought we'd have more time with you. I continue to pray, as you've taught me, to provide me with some rationale as to how we got here, how this spot on your "dash" is supposed to be entwined with the Mom we know, fun-loving, always laughing, engaging, resilient, and inspirational, and it just doesn't seem to fit the mold. And then I remember, this is our time to reflect, share memories, encourage you, and help carry you through this, as you would do.

Now I have to ask myself, how will I ever "fill those big shoes?" I love you, Mom. What an honor to help fill your dash.

CHAPTER SIX

When Time Stopped

—

The ALS diagnosis came as a shock, and I know it was to her as well. Upon hearing this diagnosis, I immediately began trying to discount it. Surely, they were all wrong. What did they miss in their assessment? What did I miss in mine? I began reaching out to ALS specialists who authored articles on ALS, emailing them as not many had resumed office hours due to the pandemic. I reached out to the founder of the ALS Clinic at Johns Hopkins, as I needed more information, someone to tell me that this can't be reality.

The following is the email I sent:

> My mom, age 79, was just diagnosed with ALS. This does not run in our family, which, from my research, only accounts for some causes of ALS onset. Prior to her ALS diagnosis, doctors began treating her for Myasthenia Gravis using plasmapheresis. She presented with slurred speech, difficulty swallowing, and breathing issues, i.e., "running out of breath." She has asthma and uses an inhaler twice a day. She fit the profile for Myasthenia Gravis and did show improvement with the treatment; breathing is better, and her slurred speech is gone. She does

exhibit dysphagia symptoms.

She has had a difficult year, including spinal surgery to correct scoliosis and nerve compression (leading to a drop foot on her right foot). The surgery was successful, but she developed blood clots in both of her legs and one pulmonary embolism, which was treated with Eloquis. After surgery, she completed acute rehab, returned home, and was getting stronger, and her drop foot was beginning to move again. She then fell after tripping over a ramp and broke her leg. Again, spending time in a nursing home (short-term rehab), lying in a bed, as she was non-weight bearing for several weeks. During her stay at the nursing home, she was getting physical therapy, riding the stationary bike, lifting weights, and adjusting.

Which brings me to why I'm emailing you. I am having a difficult time understanding the ALS diagnosis for several reasons: her age of diagnosis, and the noticeable improvement in her walking two months ago after surgery. The breathing, swallowing, and speech issues did not present until a month ago. Would ALS symptoms come on rapidly? Are there other diseases or conditions that she could have, such as Guillain-Barré Syndrome or Polymyositis? She has had MRIs, "cookie swallow" tests, blood work, EMG tests, x-rays, and more.

I am sorry for the lengthy email, but she is everything to me, and I am feeling deflated and quite surprised by this sudden diagnosis. Could we be missing something? I did some reading and researched ALS, and saw your name, and I was hoping you could help me.

I also discovered that the disease appears more predominantly in men, and the age range of the onset of symptoms can be anywhere from 40 to 70 years. This did not fit my mom's scenario. (End of email)

This doctor kindly took the time to respond to my email, and thus began my learning curve with this awful disease. The age range is 18 to 99 years (average age of diagnosis is 50 to 60 years), and 90% of cases are sporadic, not familial, meaning this is more likely to strike people who do not inherit it from family members. After receiving this email, I continued to discount this doctor's response. Her symptoms could point to other conditions, just not ALS, kept circling in my mind. Reflecting on this moment, I recalled my mom mentioning other strange symptoms that she was experiencing– leg cramps, muscle twitches, and she was beginning to have more falls, resulting in X-rays and ER visits. This doctor referred me to an ALS specialist in our area whom we could see. My learning curve was just beginning despite my desire to avoid this lesson.

The second opinion, based on the Johns Hopkins doctor's referral and subsequent opinions, was undeniable. I had asked for prayers prior to the appointment, and I often wondered, looking back now, whether they were heard. I couldn't see past the sorrow to see this, as she never gave up on her fight, and we were only beginning to watch her courage unfold. Unable to see her in person, I began going through my memories and reviewing old photographs of our lives. I created a Facebook page dedicated to encouraging her without being there in person. I asked family members and friends to post notes of encouragement and fun memories to lift her spirits. What I witnessed through this act was how many lives she has impacted. She had touched many in a way that most could only hope to during their lifetimes.

This was the beginning of our new "normal" with ALS. There were prescriptions to be filled, such as Riluzole, a Bi-PAP breathing mask, more testing to monitor swallowing capabilities, and reaching out to ALS contacts. One of those contacts happened to be with the ALS Association Northern Ohio Chapter. What a divine blessing and difference this call would prove to be for us. There were motorized wheelchairs to order, hospital beds, bedside commodes, therapies, and at-home health aides. Her vital lung capacity, or FVC, was measured several times a day, and I researched clinical trials, such as the Healey Platform trial and others at The Ohio State University's ALS clinic. Unfortunately, she did not qualify for any clinical trials due to the advanced stage of the disease. I promised to keep on fighting and searching for answers.

Other items that needed to be investigated included voice banking, message banking, and getting a speech-language pathologist involved. As I learned, voice and message banking were techniques that can be used before ALS robs someone of their voice. The voice banking process requires recording common phrases and words so they can be used in the future to communicate.

It was all we could do to digest this new "normal," then we'd be thrown another blow. There was a new drug at the time, AMX0035, that did provide some hope, but it was still awaiting FDA approval. Studies showed that this drug lessened the effects of ALS, not cured it, but allowed patients the opportunity to live a little longer. I'll take it!

The ALS specialists advocated for a discharge into an acute rehab facility, as it was imperative that Mom continue to work on keeping her joints limber, moving, and working with a speech pathologist. Medicare denied this twice, stating that she would not benefit from this type of facility. Instead, approved the transfer back to the nursing home that she had "graduated" a month ago (this, in itself, is motivation for another journal!).

In early November, she was discharged back to the nursing home facility. We were desperate to have her with us and not isolated again, but it was a matter of the care we could provide that gave us all pause. So, while she endured another stay, we scrambled to find ways to bring her home where she would feel safe and "not be a burden," as she put it, to all of us.

She was scheduled for PEG (Percutaneous Endoscopic Gastrostomy) tube surgery, as her swallowing had made it difficult to eat, and she was losing more weight and more strength. This surgery involves inserting a tube into the stomach through which nutrients can be administered when patients cannot adequately achieve this orally. The ALS Specialist stated that this surgery would be necessary in her advanced stage of ALS due to the struggle to eat, drink, and swallow, and she was losing strength and weight. In addition to these struggles, she was experiencing more difficulty with breathing, and the doctor felt that the surgery should be performed now instead of later to give her a better chance at handling the surgery and anesthesia in this state. I was terrified at the thought of never seeing her again, but she agreed to the surgery. She was discharged to the apartment prior to the surgery, and I immediately made the trip to see her.

There were also many questions and steps that needed to be in place once the surgery was completed. We made calls, organized our thoughts, and proceeded with a plan. Who would handle the PEG feedings and wound care? Who would provide the training necessary to administer the PEG feedings, such as how to prepare the nutrients, and could she still eat soft foods, such as eggs and mashed potatoes? In addition to having this tube surgery, how would we monitor for infection at the surgical site? In addition to these surgery questions, there were other concerns that arose. Would OT/PT and speech continue when she moved to the independent living apartment? How would we arrange help with bathing and dressing her in the apartment? I wrote the following letter to her after digesting the news about her upcoming surgery.

November 21, 2020

Dearest Mom,

I wanted to express to you just what you mean to me, just in case you weren't already aware! I love thinking about our upbringing, so many fun memories and life lessons that you have imparted to me along the way. Your strength and wisdom have no end, and you've provided me with so much inspiration that it is difficult to put into words. But I will give it a try!

I remember always being in awe of you, someone I always admired and felt blessed to have in my corner. Oftentimes, I hear others say how lucky I am to have you, such a beautiful soul, inside and out. At times, I caught myself being envious at the joy you resonated when you walked into a room full of strangers, only to endear yourself to everyone you came into contact with, whether it was a softball game, piano recital, or school event. I could always count on you to have my back, cheering from the sidelines while exhibiting your pride in all of us. You gently let us make mistakes while ensuring that we learned the lesson. You provided us with so many opportunities to dream and pursue our passions. You are the epitome of what every mother and human should aspire to be in life.

When I got married, it seemed only fitting to share that dance with you. It is because you loved me that I am the person I am today, and I am forever grateful for that. Every step I took in life, you encouraged, supported, and believed in me.

When I had children of my own, what a blessing and an honor to have you provide guidance and advice, along with your own injection of humor, along the way. I remember thinking at one time that I would do things differently with my own kids, only to revert back to how I was raised. And the more my children grew, I realized what a compliment it was to hear my children say, "You're just like Nana," such music to my ears! I loved watching you play with the kids when they were little, getting them ice cream every night during their visits, exciting trips, and spoiling them, as grandparents do. And how much fun they had visiting with you and Grampa during the summer breaks, each one spending days with you two. In fact, they would start asking when they were going in February! They have not outgrown that time with you guys, even as they got older, such a blessing, and only confirms what I have known all my life, spending time with you is always enjoyable. In fact, we always leave wanting more!

I have a multitude of photographs that capture so many memories. As I look into each one, I am transported back to the time of the photo, laughing, recalling the memories when the camera lens clicked. Some days, I wish we could go back to those and extend the time a little longer in that moment. These are just some of the many times when these enjoyable marks are left on my life, along *with so many moments not captured by a camera lens. Full of love and laughter.*

You are my blessing and my joy, all mixed together in love. I am so honored to be your daughter and think of you as one of my best friends. From milestones, birthdays, vacations, and board games to hour-long phone calls, I wouldn't change a thing. You have achieved what every parent aspires to achieve: happy children, loving grandchildren, and a truly remarkable and wonderful imprint on all those who know you!

I love you with all of my heart. Thank you for filling it!

CHAPTER SEVEN

The Power of Positivity

—

I arrived to see her prior to her PEG surgery, slated for Thanksgiving week. My kids made the trip with me, wearing masks for our visit, and I brought two boogie boards (*writing tablets*) to help her communicate since she had drastically lost the ability to speak, between the slurred speech and breathing. I remember bending to give her a hug as she sat in her chair when we arrived, dropping everything in my arms just to get to her as I entered through the door. She smiled, as she always did, when we arrived. Instinctively, I reached for her hand, as I always did. I quickly noticed the strong grip of her hand in mine, and a sense of peace came over me as I realized she still had an inner strength that gave energy to our silence.

I remember how Mike, the youngest, drove all the way from North Carolina to surprise her that night, as I know he felt the same feelings and apprehension that we all did about the upcoming surgery. She cried at the sight of him walking through the door as he leaned in for a hug. Although crying was difficult for her at this stage of the disease due to the issues with her breathing, the emotions got the better of her in the moment, and she resorted to quietly calming her astonishment. Her reaction to having us with her once again was apparent, as her smile and joy lit up the room.

She thoroughly enjoyed getting her hair curled by my daughter, while laughter and conversations filled that small space. Although unseen, the presence of uneasiness and anxiety also filled the space, but we were busy forcing it out with our love and admiration for her. We reluctantly wrapped up the evening as she showed signs of exhaustion, knowing that the bedtime routine would surely take its toll.

Two days later, we received news that the surgery was finished, and we awaited the time to come and see her again. Up until now, I had her focus on what she can do and not on what she can't do anymore, in my lame attempt to keep her spirit strong. Little did I know how strong her spirit would prevail in the months to come. I wrote this poem for her to remind her of what she could mentally do and not to focus on her ever-evolving physical limitations.

December 5, 2020

I Can

What I can do is...

...brighten every room without the use of lights.

...overcome life's challenges with the power of my faith and the beauty of my grace.

...use my strength and wisdom to voice my thoughts, even if I appear silent.

...continue to persevere and believe in my abilities despite what others might think.

...rise above my darkest moments with purpose and stand tall in my determination.

...dance with joy at my blessings, defying my aging body.

...display my enthusiasm for living, undeterred by my weakness.

...feel the love of those around me and smile, knowing my love has no limits.

What I can do is continue to inspire those who love me, showcase my courage to those who are strangers, and find peace with all the lives that I have impacted.

There is no limit to my resolve.

I love you, Mom!

CHAPTER EIGHT

Christmas Surprise

———

She arrived home after the PEG surgery at the beginning of December 2020, learning to adjust to her new way of obtaining nutrients and food. Along with learning to prepare her feedings, as well as recovering, she continued to amaze us with her resilience. My visits continued, with me making the four-hour trip several times a week to see her, and were now becoming more routine and purposeful. Her voice was becoming weaker, and I remarked that I had to see her in person to ease my soul.

I was busy trying to make the approaching holiday and life in general, a little more bearable. I contacted a local wheelchair van rental agency to fulfill a promise that I had made to her (and myself) a few weeks prior. I wanted to take her back to visit our house, which she believed she would never get to return to. I knew the importance and meaning of this to her heart, and to mine, for that matter. I wanted her to have the opportunity to say goodbye to those blessed walls that made up our lives, and to the memories created in that beautiful place. Birthday parties, penciled growth charts on door jams, high school graduations, and a grandchild's sanctuary are only a few. After getting the information from the rental agency, I planned the date I would arrive. I researched local Christmas light displays to visit during this trip, since I knew how much she enjoyed looking at the lights of Christmas. My kids and I arranged the driving, as I would need our oldest son to follow us in our minivan once I picked up the rental, since we could not all fit inside it. I coordinated with Gene on the timing so that Mom would be ready for the surprise when we arrived. In addition, I had scheduled a time for a few of her friends from our old neighborhood to situate themselves outside their houses with posters of inspiration and support to greet us as we entered our old neighborhood. Since the pandemic had made visiting and seeing people impossible, we assembled a small group to hold signs in the event that she might want to stop and see some familiar faces. I made some of her favorite Christmas cookies and packed some yogurt, a food she could tolerate if she got hungry during our time at the house. We finally had our plan.

The day arrived, and we made our way to pick up the rental van. My kids each chose to dress up in Christmas outfits to bring joy and laughter. Our oldest son wore a Santa hat, our middle son wore an elf costume (one of her favorite Christmas movies), and our youngest daughter wore a reindeer outfit. I wore a Santa hat as well, and we brought an elf hat for Gene and a Santa hat for Mom. After picking up the rental van, the kids followed me in our van, and we arrived at the independent living apartment. She was dressed and ready, and I remember explaining the trip that we had planned. She laughed at her grandchildren's outfits, as she loved to laugh and enjoy moments such as these. She could not understand how she could ride in a car with the wheelchair, and I explained that we rented a special van for this adventure. She was astonished and surprised, and I could sense her joy and concern combined. We wheeled her outside to the wheelchair van, complete with a giant red bow I had borrowed from a friend resting on the roof. She could not believe her eyes, and she silently choked back tears once outside. Once she was secured inside, I told her of our plan to take her home for a visit and to see Christmas lights. She softly whispered her concern about how she would manage to get inside the house, and I explained that we would all lift her chair to help her inside. Once we were off, we talked about how nice it was to have a joy ride, not one to a doctor's appointment or hospital. I am sure she had moments of anxiety during this drive, since my navigational skills needed some work, but when I glanced in the mirror, she was smiling and happily glancing out the window. How nice for her to enjoy seeing the outside world once again.

When we approached the neighborhood, our willing group had gathered in the yard holding up posters of support and funny wishes. She was once again surprised and could not contain her excitement as we pulled into their driveway to wave and see familiar faces that she hadn't seen in months. I was able to convey her thoughts and comments, as her voice was more of a whisper, as they arrived at the car window to share their joy in seeing her once again. We collected and placed the posters in the van after our short visit, as I knew this trip would exhaust her. We then made our way to our house and wheeled her inside. I think she was achingly aware of the memories of our lives here, and she told me the history behind some of our family artifacts and photographs that were displayed on the bookshelves in the family room. We laughed about some of the memories we had lovingly created in these rooms, then moved our conversation to the kitchen, where we enjoyed some cookies and yogurt. We helped her move into the living room, where our piano resided. So many duets played between us on that piano! It was as if she were recalling that same memory along with me, and she attempted to raise her arm to the keys to play along with me. I sensed her desire to play again, so I helped place her arm up to the keys. Somehow, we managed to play a little section of the song "Heart and Soul" together, one that we had played so many times during our lives. That will always be one of my many memorable moments with her.

We wanted to see the Christmas lights and knew the exhaustion of this trip would soon settle in for her, so we reluctantly said our goodbyes to our house full of memories and returned to the van. I desperately wanted to stay in that house longer with her, but I knew her bedtime routine was quickly approaching, and how tired she would be after our adventure. I drove us past lights set to music and the hometown city Christmas light display. Seeing the joy and awe in her eyes was worth the drive and time spent this day. We returned her home to the apartment, complete with the cookies and posters, and said our goodbyes, as we had to return the rental van and then make our trip back home for the night. I am forever grateful for having that time with her.

Reflecting on this time, I approached each visit without hesitation, as it meant that I could hug her, see her smile, and hold her hand, all while trying to inspire her strength. I continued to reach out to facilities and researchers in the field to obtain new information and enroll her in clinical trials, as I so much wanted her to "beat the odds" of this disease, or at the very least, remain with us a little longer. You see, at age 79, I was still not ready to let her go. I still needed my mom.

And with each visit, we always left smiling.

December 16, 2020

Always Leave Smiling

I watch as everyone is gearing up for the holiday season, quickly approaching, and like most, memories of traditions, get-togethers, and celebrating with family and friends are in the forefront. And for many, this year is different. Traditions and celebrations were replaced by virtual gatherings, and so many of us were missing family members or friends, and some were stumbling through a holiday season without a loved one.

And yet there are some of us dealing with a toned-down celebration, unable to gather or visit compromised loved ones either in nursing homes or battling a terminal disease. I am experiencing the latter as one of my favorite people, my mom, has been recently diagnosed with Amyotrophic Lateral Sclerosis, or ALS. What impacts me the most is the utter determination and endurance she displays. The mundane events that I take for granted, walking to the kitchen to find something to eat, washing or combing my hair, and getting dressed, are appreciated that much more. Going for a drive to wrap my head around life, voicing my opinion or providing encouragement to someone, and putting myself to bed at night are some of the many tasks that I used to take for granted. How did we get here?

For those who endure this horrific disease, you lose so much of your abilities and grapple with your new way of life. You find your once able-bodied self now relying on others every moment in your day, humility discarded, and you heartbreakingly accept that your independence is challenged. ALS attacks the motor neurons, progressively affecting muscles throughout your body. Only 10% of those diagnosed with ALS have a family history; 90% are sporadic. The age range of the disease is 18 – 99 years. There is no known cure. What I wish I didn't know about this disease, but now find myself discovering organizations, services, doctors, and clinical trials. This does not affect your mind, and I know you are still Mom. I miss our hour-long phone calls, your laugh, and your voice. I helplessly watch the progression, but you, beautiful you, live it. Through it all, you find humor, grace, resilience, and strength. We focus on what you CAN do and not what you CAN'T, as positivity is the key to your resolve. You find joy in what you can do, smile at what you've accomplished in life, and find the life lessons when we ourselves struggle with the material. Mom, you have always been the best teacher that I have known, ensuring we learn that each stumble brings valuable experiences. Each life lesson entails unique instruction and can be taught with different techniques, but each lesson requires intense focus. Some lessons need more explanation, and some we may never understand, but I have learned to never give up hope. After all, what a waste of instruction if we never gain the knowledge. A genuine hug is always a gift, a hearty laugh will never be taken for granted, and hearing you say "I love you" will always be music to my ears.

ALS might be the abbreviation for our new chapter in the life manual, but I will _Always _Leave _Smiling (ALS) after time spent with you, Mom. And I will remember this lesson, not fondly, but for what you have taught me during this. Never give up hope, cherish your blessings, and continue to be the brightest presence in the room. I have always been present during the course of life, but what I would give to retake the course a few more times with you. I love your strength, your gift of joy, and all the blessings you have given to me over the years. I love everything about you, too, Mom.

/ CHAPTER NINE

Photographs

—

The Christmas holiday was quickly approaching, as was my desire to spend more time with her. Each visit, I would tease her that this was like the 12 days of Christmas, surprising her with gifts each time. In the earlier part of December, we brought an artificial Christmas tree, complete with trimmings, to their apartment. The look on her face when we arrived with a tree in tow brought joy to my face, as I watched my kids arrange the tree, complete with lights and ornaments, for her to have in their new space. I knew the importance of setting this up for her, as in the back of my mind, I had contemplated that this might be her last Christmas with us. Everything had to be festive and bright, after all, she deserved all of this and more. In addition, my younger brother, Mike, had brought over some Christmas boxes from our house to fill in memories of past Christmases.

We also determined that more help was needed for her care, as Gene could not attempt this task alone. After interviewing several recommended home health care agencies, we secured one, albeit one that was fraught with issues. On some days, an aide would show up late or not at all. Other days, the aide would arrive without the necessary training to help her with everyday tasks, such as helping Mom to the bathroom using the Sara Stedy. The other concern was aides not using a mask during their shifts, as Mom could not properly wear one without compromising her already weakened state.

We were gearing up to sell the house, as we anticipated that she could no longer thrive there with all of the steps. I remember the baseball games my brothers would host in the backyard, the intimate dinners, the conversations and laughter that filled the kitchen, holiday gatherings, surprise parties, duets on the piano, and so many more memories that filled those walls. So, in between packing up our memories, we were all reliving our lives spent in that house. To say it was an undertaking was putting it lightly, as every trip up to see Mom was divided between my desire to spend time with her and also focusing on the task at hand, which was packing.

I spent weeks driving up to pack a lifetime of memories in boxes and then rush to spend a few hours visiting with Mom. We used this time visiting to provide a break for Gene, and her, and relive memories that had found their way into boxes lovingly retrieved from the house. So many photographs filled those boxes, and I was anxious to make sure that I would appreciate the love of the moment behind every picture. Each visit, she would write on her boogie board tablet about a specific moment, as if reliving it in her head, as her mind always remained intact and on point throughout her diagnosis. I often think about how that must have felt for her, to still be inside a body that no longer performed as normal. Photographs are purposeful for that reason, allowing us to relive memories and take us back to the moments they were captured.

December 21, 2021

Mom,

As you know, I always find solace in writing, which I find myself doing a lot these days! I have been spending time going through pictures lately, which are strewn about in front of me, with some etched in my mind. I know you have asked yourself, as I have, why me? Why are you the one facing this dreadful disease? Why are you the one having to navigate this path? Why oh why did this happen during a pandemic when we have to keep our distance, wear masks that hide our joy, unable to kiss your beautiful face? These are some of the many questions that go through my head while I look through my life with you.

There is one picture that keeps resurfacing in my head. In the photo, you are seated behind me, and we're wearing matching dresses that you made for us. I think I must have been about five years old, and it was a light peach dress with a large collar, and taken at our first house in the front room. I'm not sure why this image stands out to me right now, clearly visible in my mind. In the photo, you have your hair done, as you always do, and you look so proud and happy, as mothers do. Your gaze rests on my young, impish grin. Your smile radiates in the simple joy of celebrating the moment. I have the sides of my hair upswept in a clip, my curls circling my childish face. I don't remember who took the picture or why. Maybe it was to capture the moment of a mother and daughter in matching dresses? Even from the photo, it is clear that you inspire and create warmth, happiness, and love. We are blissfully content in that moment, and it is so eloquently captured by the camera lens. And yet, the photo seems to also capture your courage, determination, and a joyful commanding presence. Recalling the photo in my mind pulsates with joy, and it is clear that your gift spreads beyond the two of us in the photo. In fact, I can sense the love felt by the photographer in capturing the moment. You are so young in the photo, and I am reminded of so much possibility that resides in that photo, from your perspective on making sure I grow up happy to my perspective of will I always find happiness?

I think about those years and so many years in between that photo and now, what a wonderful life! And we still somehow coordinate matching outfits after all of these years. In fact, I remember showing up at events and discovering that we'd chosen similar outfits, completely unplanned! It is as if we think alike or have a mother/daughter psychic ability. I smile when I recall spending the day shopping with just the two of us at the outlet mall, a spur-of-the-moment decision before I headed back to my house. We cherished our time, going from store to store, sharing laughs and opinions. In that moment, it was as if it were just the two of us, no other customers existed, and we embraced the sheer spontaneity we created. We were so excited when we found matching sweaters and impulsively purchased them so we could be "twins." And ending that day full of giggles, nestled at a table, with bottles of water, and sharing a warm pretzel, analyzing how we would transport our armful of bags to our cars. I will always have that day with you, creating wonderful memories and thoroughly enjoying every moment of that day.

It is from you that I have learned to approach life without hesitation and welcome newer paths regardless of who is watching, just create with conviction and determination. Be strong in your pursuit of your dreams and consider last-minute changes as opportunities. You have exhibited more courage during your lifetime that one cannot help but pay attention and learn the lessons you have provided. If you only knew the impact of your grace, determination, and love in all of our lives. You make each of us better people by knowing you, and more grateful for loving you.

And then it dawns on me why that picture from when I was a child resonates with me. It pinpoints a time in my life when I was happy, secure, and loved, not a care in the world, and ignorant of life's imperfections. A moment captured by a camera lens, defining emotions and security, all provided under your watchful eye. And now, here we are, so many years later, and I'm happy, secure, and loved, as I was when that lens clicked. The confidence that you showcased in that photo has now been imprinted in me, and the happiness has spread not only to the two of us in the picture but to everyone in our lives. Your light is special and continues to touch all of those around you.

So, now when I ask why? I think the answer lies within that photo.

CHAPTER TEN

Losing Your Voice

—

We spent Christmas Eve using our Echo Show, a technology-enhancing feature that was utilized and appreciated during the pandemic, to converse with Mom, along with Bud's family and Mike's family. It was somewhat difficult with so many of us sharing the screen, as when one group started talking, it was difficult to hear the others. Mom, especially, had trouble communicating with us, as it was increasingly more difficult for her to speak. It was not at all what we had enjoyed in the past, but we were able to see each other, and we took comfort in that. I had planned to drive up the next morning with my family for Christmas, as I needed to spend this last Christmas with her in person. However, once I awoke, it was clear that we would not be able to drive to see her, as it had snowed considerably the night before. A white Christmas is what many of us anticipate, watching the snow glide softly to the ground, coating the branches of trees covered in a glistening calm. However, this Christmas morning was different for me. I was crushed and heartbroken. I tried to come to terms with the fact that maybe there was some reason I was not meant to be there with Mom on this day, although for the life of me, I will never comprehend that reason. We arranged for us to come for a visit the day after Christmas, which I eagerly scheduled.

Once we arrived, I quickly assumed my routine, dropping all my belongings just to get to hug her as we entered. The apartment was adorned with Christmas decorations, and she was in a festive mood, but muted compared to other times. Past Christmases were spent with my mom and Gene traveling down to see family and awakening to the joys of delight on Christmas morning. Breakfast casseroles and monkey bread scents filled the kitchen, wrapping paper and gifts strewn about, concealing the carpeted family room, and the excitement of visiting and playing board games was anticipated on those mornings. However, this morning, this was replaced with an aching desire to spend each minute sitting with her, holding her hand, and seeing what she would write and convey on her boogie board. She always used her right hand to write, but this gift was lost to this unrelenting disease. Recently, she began to use her non-dominant hand to convey her thoughts, and I was surprised by how well she was able to write. The boogie board became a lifeline for her to contribute to conversations held around her. I recall pausing some conversations so she could write down her thoughts, as when most of us spoke, we would verbalize quickly and continue on to the topic. Although Mom was focused on contributing, she was determined to have her voice heard. We "fought" for time next to her, as her responses were always witty, insightful, and purposeful. This "pause" was challenging for her, I believe, as she was normally the sought-after voice that filled a room, and now it was dictated by how quickly she could scribble thoughts on a board. She continued to build her strength by doing daily exercises to work her arms and hands. She would often tease us by mustering her strength to raise her fisted hand in the air, pretending to punch the nearest person, but never connecting!

We started off the new year with another virtual New Year's celebration with our Echo Show. It was convenient, and it kept her safe from exposure, but it could not replace my in-person visits, double-masked and symptom-free. The weather had shifted to cold and snow, so making the drive to visit required more planning, as it would dictate my travel arrangements much as it had during our prior visit for Christmas.

It became apparent that she was losing more of her voice. I had researched "voice banking", as well as a Tobii device, a computer/tablet that she could use to communicate. But this proved cumbersome, and learning new technology at her age was not feasible, only frustrating. I can recall how she fumbled with the technology and how to create phrases for use. Since she had lost the option of voice banking, we learned how she could use the device to type words and phrases and press a button to repeat them. We started off by typing "Gene" and had her press the button to repeat the word, and we continued to press it, much to our delight and laughter. We then typed in the phrase "massage my feet," to which she silently giggled in joyfulness. The Tobii device was amazing at providing a much-needed voice to those who had lost this gift, but it was also heavy and burdensome for her to use due to the loss of arm strength. We tried having her use her cushioned lap pad, but this proved fruitless.

I googled many caregiver grants for ALS caregivers, as providing the in-home care was now 24-hour care, as she often needed help during the night. Many places offered these types of grants, and I applied online, by phone, and by handwritten requests. Each person I spoke with at these organizations had known someone with ALS, and the conversations with them were insightful, emotional, and therapeutic. I cannot thank them enough for their thoughts, prayers, and most of all, empathy for our situation. Although I knew their empathy was unfortunately due to their own experience with ALS.

We determined that voice banking was not a viable option for her due to her increasing loss of voice and breath. I did notice, one day during a visit, that she said the phrase "how 'bout that," to which I immediately took the opportunity to celebrate with her and also record her on my phone. She seemed eager to repeat the phrase, and with focus, she was able to muster saying "I love you," which I gleefully recorded. Her voice had changed tone, and she didn't sound like the Mom from a few months earlier, but what joy this brought to my ears to hear her. When she was first diagnosed with ALS, I remember thinking how tragic and devastating this was. But losing her voice was just another compounding loss to this unrelenting disease.

January 4th, 2021

I love hearing your voice. How does a person's voice define who they are? They say the window of a person's soul is through their eyes. While I agree, I also feel that their voice contributes to their being. It makes us who we are, it differentiates us from others - our laugh, whisper, the lilt in our spoken words, sharing a joke, enthusiastic expressions and joy, accentuating specific words to convey meaning, fiercely advocating or encouraging, softly consoling or exuding empathy. A voice is our means of communicating our thoughts, dreams, happiness, pride, and love. What happens when you lose your voice? Do you lose a piece of yourself? I hate ALS. I hate what this does to those we love, especially you, mom. I hate watching this disease, but you, beautiful you, you live it. I hate that you have to endure losing elements of you — your movement, your humility, your independence, but I really hate that you lose your voice. Your guidance, silly jokes, laughter, and general conversations that I usually took for granted are now emblazoned in my head. What I wouldn't give to get one day back to hear you, one normal day is all I ask. I imagine what we would talk about in that one day, how we would prioritize our conversation, and what we would discuss. Maybe we would relive some enjoyable memories, focus on past lessons, or just sit and giggle. Maybe I would listen as you shared some memorable quotes, sing a lullaby, or provide background on old photographs. I do know that if we had "that day," I would relish every minute, as I always do. And then I realize that through all of this, you are still you, you are still mom, you are still as beautiful as you have always been. You are now even larger than life itself, as you continue to find the laughter and find your new voice. It may not be how you want to communicate, but you are still the biggest presence in the room; you are still the one I go to for acceptance and showcasing more courage than I have witnessed in my lifetime. You are still Mom. Defining someone's voice doesn't seem so imperative now, as you clearly show me that it is not always about using your voice; sometimes it is about finding a new one.

CHAPTER ELEVEN

Finding Strength
Through Lessons

The pandemic terrified us in many ways. We had to be extremely careful with her, as our fears of her getting sick would shorten her time with us even more. We had strict guidelines for visits: each of us had to be isolated at home, order our groceries and pick them up wearing a mask, have our food delivered to the apartment, and limit contact with outsiders. Appointments with doctors were viewed and attended online. Every visit with her at the apartment required a health screening for each of us, which included a temperature check, masks, and a recording sheet for all of this information. We then placed a sticker on our shirts stating our names, the room number we were visiting, the date, and our current internal temperature. There were many times during all of this when I asked myself, "How are we here?" I hate ALS, and I hate this pandemic. My mom needed support from family and friends, but instead, she was isolated from them all. She needed interaction with the outside world, visits from friends to lift her spirits, and above all, family to bring comfort, encouragement, and laughter when she needed it the most. Not only was she in the midst of this cruel disease, but she was also facing restrictions on who she could see and when. I was angry and heartbroken with her situation, but my focus was on her.

Our visits continued at her apartment, and with each visit, we obeyed the regulations for permission to see her in person. The frustration I felt with each visit was growing inside of me regarding this routine, even though I understood its importance. I just wanted to see my mom, hold her hand, and ease my soul. Will these precautions ever end? I wanted to spend the night so I could spend more time with her, but the fear of the pandemic and removing my mask in her presence persuaded me to reluctantly leave and drive home after each visit. I did not want to be the one to expose her to COVID-19 in her weakened state. Gosh, how I grappled with this rationale. I played that scene in my mind during each visit, taking off my mask and sitting with her by her bed all night. She would often motion for us to take off our masks so she could see our faces again, but the reality of making her time with us shorter kept resurfacing in my head, and our masked faces continued to greet her. I was too afraid of what could happen, and that aspect made me angry with all of this, the pandemic and COVID-19.

Finally, news broke that COVID-19 vaccines would be given to those in nursing homes. My mom and Gene agreed to sign up and have theirs done. The first dose was given in mid-January. After receiving the initial dose, they both seemed fine for the first few hours afterward, but by that evening, she began experiencing trouble breathing. My cousin was visiting at the time and recognized that she was having trouble catching her breath, and, as my cousin put it, the look in her eyes showed concern. They called for an ambulance, and my cousin, thankfully, remembered to send my mom with the boogie board so she could communicate with the paramedics and hospital staff. She was once again taken to a hospital with no visitors, and no way to verbalize her symptoms or concerns (thank goodness for the boogie board). I still am not sure what caused this reaction with the vaccine. She was given steroids and breathing treatments, as she had used an inhaler for asthma her whole life, so we attributed it to a possible cause for the reaction. Either way, she spent over a week in the hospital, without therapy, and not moving from her bed. In this weakened state, she once again made the decision to move to her previous nursing home to regain what strength she had lost due to this most recent hospitalization. It was now the beginning of February, and the relief that came with the news of a vaccine was quickly altered by her reaction to it.

It was during this time that memories of her and our time together became so vivid, spontaneous, and continuous. So many lessons were taught to me growing up, and there was still so much more I could learn from her. I will never stop yearning for those lessons and that time with her.

February 4th, 2021

Because you loved me . . .

I find joy in everyday situations and learn not to accept limitations, as the sky is the limit, and pursuing your dreams is attainable.

I can overcome life's obstacles and recognize and profit from the lessons.

I find my inner strength when needed and rely on my faith when my strength needs guidance.

I am able to laugh and spread kindness to those who would benefit and those who don't always recognize the need.

I can love fiercely and unconditionally, especially with my family, whether showcasing my blessings or advocating for a perceived injustice.

I can find humor when experiencing trials, as I have learned that laughing truly is the best medicine for dealing with life.

I recognize and believe in miracles and know that sometimes you need to be open to them, as miracles come in all shapes and sizes.

I know the importance of forgiveness and empathy and what it does to the soul.

I can use my voice to right a wrong, express happiness and offer encouragement, and console when needed.

I believe in myself and know that no challenge is insurmountable, and inspiration and courage can be found not only in people but also in how we face our most difficult situations.

I learned to always use your manners, be respectful, display sincerity in your convictions, and be open for growth as a person.

I know how compassion and listening to one's joys or problems leaves an everlasting imprint, and the importance of allowing that imprint to be a reflection of your true self.

I am who I am today, a wife, mother, aunt, sister, cousin, and friend who is grateful.

Because you loved me, I am forever blessed.

CHAPTER TWELVE

"I Miss My Life"

—

She spent more time in the nursing home, thankful for what physical therapy she was allotted, fighting with every ounce of her being to gather the strength she felt was necessary to come back to us in the independent living apartment, back with her family. I remember the phone calls between us that I used to assess her progress. I also remember continuing these calls, each lasting only a minute or two, as she "ran out of breath", as I still needed to check on her, even if only for a one-sided conversation. She conveyed her frustration over not being able to eat the food provided, as it was difficult to chew, cold, or just plain gross. She also explained that the administrators, who did not interact with her, believed she was too weak to continue using the Sara Steady, the sole device she had relied on to help her to the bathroom. They stated that she would need to consider transitioning to a Hoyer Lift, a sling transfer device. She was adamant, God bless her, and told me with whatever ounce of disdain she could assemble, that she did not want to use this, as she reverently knew she could still use the Sara Stedy. A Hoyer Lift is a harness-type device that assists those who have lost the control or ability to walk and stand. It is wrapped around their body while they lie in bed, much like a hammock. Caregivers then use a crank to lift people up into the air and move them while they lie in this "hammock," praying that they don't fall onto the floor. She absolutely hated this idea, and I think it spurred her on to prove to them that she still had the determination to maintain what dignity she had left.

One week into this stay, much like in times past, we held the usual "progress update" phone call to discuss her future goals and plans for her to either stay or be discharged. Those present on the phone were me, my mom, Gene, the social worker, the physical therapist, and the discharge nurse. I recalled hearing them tell us that she would need to move to the sling device as she could no longer pull herself up to the standing position required to use the Sara Stedy. As they talked over her, I interrupted and said that she was not comfortable using that device and preferred her normal means of transportation. I asked them to talk with one of her nurses who took care of her because my mom said this nurse could attest to her strength in using the Sara Stedy. My voice became hers in a continual campaign to help her. The group suggested that I consider coming to receive training on this new transfer device in the event we would need to resort to it. I knew she would not give up the fight for her freedom of choices in the matter, but I also recall how excited I was because I would be allowed in to see her. My mom and I both agreed to pursue the training, as we both knew what a visit meant to us. I was looking forward to seeing her again in person, and I also knew this indicated that she would be released soon and able to come back to the apartment.

We had not been able to see her in person for a few weeks, and I found myself struggling to sleep the night before the visit. I was anticipating the training using the Hoyer Lift, knowing that it was "not in the cards" with my mom's persistence. At the same time, I had put this training in the back of my mind and surrendered to the giddiness filling my heart just to see her again. Lingering questions slowly crept into my head. Had my mom lost more strength since I had last seen her? Would I know how to help her? Could I hold her hand again, or had she lost that ability to grip my hand in hers?

When I arrived at the independent living apartment with my kids, we were met by my aunts (my mom's two sisters) and Gene. Due to the pandemic, her younger sister had not been able to travel because of the COVID-19 concerns and the restrictions. However, months into the pandemic, she was now able to make the trip. My mom's older sister had been able to visit regularly, which improved my mom's spirit with each visit and also provided my aunt with a sense of peace, being able to see her in person, much like it did for me. So, with precautions in place, we all arrived at the nursing home. Gene, my two aunts, and my kids remained outside and walked around the building to the window to her room. I complied with the routine that I had followed from previous visits, temperature checks with a date and time stamp. This time, however, I was able to venture inside the nursing home and find her room. Her face lit up as I entered. I was hopeful that my mask did not hide my anticipation and emotions, as I could feel myself rushing across the room to her for a hug. She was sitting in a chair, dressed in a light pink sweatshirt and looking beautiful, as always. She was makeup-free, which would never have happened when the company was arriving in years past. It took me back to memories where she would greet us at the door, in a loud, welcoming voice, "Hi," and her outfits always flattering on her small frame (she would love that I used the term "small" when referring to her size, as she was always conscious of being healthy). Her face, eloquently accentuated with makeup, made her blue eyes and bright smile illuminate the space.

Only today was different from those prior years, and I admired how, even with her sweatshirt attire and lack of makeup, she was glowing as she always did. I was limited on my visit, so our training got started. I witnessed how weak she had become since my last in-person visit, but I was not ready to give in to resignation in her battle. She appeared to struggle more with using her hands, arms, and legs as she welcomed me into the room. With assistance from the nurse, we moved my mom into the adjoining room to her hospital bed, her new normal area to sleep. We went through the training using the Hoyer Lift sling, a device with which I was not comfortable using for her. The nurse showed me how to place the sling under her while she was on her bed, helping her adjust so it would slip underneath her. The nurse then proceeded to use a crank of sorts to slowly lift my mom in this sling into the air for a transfer to a chair. I could tell from the look on her face as her eyes grew wide that giving up all control using this was not at all what she would consider. I couldn't say I blamed her.

After our training, we had a few minutes before I would be asked to leave. Time was, once again, not my friend. I opened the blinds to her window so she could glimpse our family standing outside. Then I quickly retrieved my cell phone to contact them, as they waited outside so they could talk to her, and assisted by dictating what she said in response to their conversation.

February 5th, 2021

As I sat with you in your room at the nursing home, to be trained on how to accompany your weakened body, we had the opportunity to visit with other family members who appeared at your window. I was there to learn how to assist you with everyday tasks that so many of us take for granted. We were blessed to have the chance for you to see your family, eager to converse with you. Several things struck me during this quick visit at the window. Initially, someone mentioned that they missed you and they were looking forward to seeing you soon. You smiled back at them, turned to me, and said in your soft-spoken, sometimes difficult to understand speech, "I miss my life."

As the somewhat one-sided conversation continued, I began to notice other little nuances that are not so little in terms of your life. Yes, your voice and ability to express your ideas, share a joke, and discuss your feelings appear muffled and silent. A head nod, a thumbs-up, and a wink are vital to your communication skills. Just positioning yourself upright in your hospital bed is met with struggle and the need for assistance. You need time to digest the conversation, sometimes missing parts of it, so that you can write down thoughts on your boogie board. Your legs and the power to walk and dance are no longer part of the equation. But the beautiful hands that you use for communicating and writing are your voice, and what I find myself constantly reaching for to express my feelings. What strikes me the most is how different the world is on the opposite side of that glass window. This thin, clear, sturdy piece of glass holds two different worlds. Watching you intently, I begin to notice how these differences play a role in your life, how you are forced to live and exist in the two different worlds daily. In your world, you are subjected to focus on all the tasks you can no longer participate in, and it seems so obvious to me now. But I am also keenly aware of your presence in this world, your radiant smile, your eyes dancing with emotion, and the fierce resolve exhibited in your existence. I am also reminded of all the things you can do and your unwavering desire to be in the moment. How can this small piece of glass separate these two distinctly different scenarios? They should be intertwined with each other; that is the way life is supposed to be, isn't it?

I reach and grab both of your hands in mine and tell you that we are not giving up on you. We are not going anywhere, and we are in this with you. But we are not, not anywhere close to it. In fact, from my point of view at the current moment, we are all located on the other side of this glass. But please know this: although you might see reflections of the "other" world, we are fighting to get to you inside your world. We will do everything in our power to help you and continue our love for you, even if we have to break that glass to do it.

CHAPTER THIRTEEN

Unyielding Spirit

—

She moved back to the independent living apartment in the middle of February 2021 and celebrated with our family. Due to the pandemic and COVID-19 concerns, family members were restricted from visiting those in nursing homes and independent living apartments. However, we discovered that if we declared hospice for her, the rules and regulations were modified due to the patient's situation. We researched hospice care, but I made it clear to my mom that by declaring this, I was in no way giving up on her and her undeniable spirit. Enrolling in hospice, as we learned, was a way that we could visit her in person, have access to nurse visits, 24-hour access to call for help if needed, and an on-call doctor to help in the event she needed medications. However, we did discover that by declaring hospice, her prescription for Rilozole, the ALS medication that was to "give her more time" with us, would be an expense that would no longer be covered with insurance. The reasoning behind this policy was that Rilozole was deemed a medication that prolonged survival (if you can even believe those terms - survival and ALS - together), and enrolling in hospice focused more on the comfort of care when near the end of life. It's ironic to me that comfort care is provided for a diagnosis such as ALS, but it does not cover medications to give an ounce of hope, and I attempted to reason with hospice on this, to no avail.

When we enrolled her in hospice, this was a detail that I had not considered. We knew that she was fighting an uphill battle, but Rilozole did provide some hope in giving her "more time" with us, and without assistance in paying for this expensive medication (as futile as it may appear to hospice policies), we were angry.

She also began experiencing multiple urinary tract infections (UTIs), attributed to lack of movement, I can only assume. But with each UTI, she had to experience conveying this to the home care team of caregivers, which was difficult in itself, with no voice. Thank goodness her mind was intact, and she was still able to scribble on her boogie board. Reflecting on this time, I can only imagine how frustrating and debilitating all this must have been for her, having her mind unchanged but her body not cooperating.

February 19th, 2021

A personal legacy is to live a life that serves as an example of what an exceptional life can look like. How many of us can attest to that definition? Are we all living a life that impacts others in a positive, enriching, compassionate way? I consider myself blessed if I have had the privilege to know someone who fits this description. And yet, here I find myself describing my mom, achingly aware of her impact on not only our family but to all of those who know her or those who have had the honor of meeting her. You see, to just casually meet her will leave you wanting to know her better, to become part of her close circle of friends in the hopes that you can benefit from her beautiful legacy.

When I was younger, I did not appreciate what I saw unfolding before my eyes, someone who took the time to listen, really listen, to those around her. She always had a way of reaching each soul and honestly caring about their life. I remember helping families in need, taking the time to visit and talk with them, and hoping that our time helped them in some way. There were phone calls to neighbors and acquaintances, always sincerely checking in with them, even when our lives were busy with activities, dinners to prepare, school events, and more. All of these instances did not go by unnoticed. These "little" things made an impact on me, although at the time, seemed mundane and time-consuming.

Reflecting on this now, I realize how important that imprint on those we care about and those we might not know very well can change a life. Looking from the inside out, I could not begin to appreciate what I was lovingly a part of, what became a part of who I am, and what I strive to be. I see this now, as I am older, and realize the importance of giving everyone your best, your true self, keeping yourself on the "list" but also engaging with those you meet, as everyone benefits from kindness and compassion. What a beautiful example of how to live your life. And I am blessed with having first-hand knowledge of how a legacy is achieved and created. Always give of your time and be truly thankful for what you have, even during times when you are not feeling like being thankful. Know that everyone has a story and challenges, and remember that when dealing with stressful encounters. Leave others wanting more of your time, laughter, and empathy, and not focusing on schedules. Always be present in the moment, for only God knows the length of your journey. Approach challenges and hardships with grace and focus on our blessings, as we ourselves become stronger after the storm. Always be open for the life lessons that are thrown our way, as this helps us become a better version of ourselves. A personal legacy is not always what we are given; it is what we can achieve when we learn from the past. Thank you for providing the foundations for all of us; we are truly better people by loving you.

CHAPTER FOURTEEN
She Was Still Mom

—

Many changes were happening in her life, along with the ALS and pandemic, she had to prepare to sell the house she had purchased 45 years ago to raise her family. So many memories in that home, raising three children by herself for many years, countless Christmas mornings, birthday celebrations, her marriage to Gene, graduations, our own marriages, grandkids, and picnics. That home was filled with so much love, it burst at the seams of those walls. And now it was time to pack up all of those memories and move her into a condo. The condo offered single-level living with two bedrooms and a larger bathroom to accommodate the wheelchair. I can only imagine how difficult this all was for her, not to be able to box up her memories, taking intimate care of each unique object, as each one represented a time in her life that only she can recall. My, how her life changed with the ALS diagnosis. All of the plans she must have made were cruelly altered. I am so sorry. I only wish I could have taken all of this away from her.

I also began writing her obituary at her request. It was heartbreaking and challenging, and I believe I was in denial as I wrote it. But with her "edits," we finished it together. We communicated by email and, as crazy as it sounds, I looked forward to each revision since it meant I could read something she wrote, her sense of humor and wit coming through each exchange.

February 24th, 2021

A Day in the Life

After a sleepless night consisting of tossing and turning and having to use the restroom, you awake. However, the tossing and turning is not achieved alone; you require assistance with every move of your body, just to get comfortable. You require every bit of your strength to press a button for help using a bedpan to relieve your aching bladder. You begin each day unable to sit up until someone can provide time to prop you upright. And even more time asking for help to get you dressed, as putting on clothes is no longer the indulgence you once anticipated. Humility and privacy are completely discarded. Your reflection in the mirror is a surprise to you as you witness what ALS has done to your body.

Attention then turns to satisfying the hunger you feel, but preparing food for yourself is no longer on the table, so to speak. PEG feedings provide your daily nutrition and the dryness that engulfs your mouth, satisfied with the ice chips fed to you because swallowing liquids is a luxury you can no longer afford. You crave a routine, which dictates how your day will go today. Once dressed, you are transferred to a stand assist to begin the long day of using all of your strength each time you feel the need to use the bedside commode, as using a toilet is no longer part of your equation. Putting on makeup and combing your hair, what used to be a daily ritual, are the highlights of the day, usually only attempting the latter, with assistance, of course. Your "can-do" attitude has abruptly adjusted to requiring assistance with every hour of your day. The hours you used to give for volunteering, fundraising for charities, and counseling others have been replaced with begrudgingly asking others for more of their time to aid in your daily tasks.

And throughout all of this, you sit in your chair, your mind and soul unchanged, your thoughts run vividly through your head as you fumble with your only means of communication. You have lots to share, memories to relive, jokes to laugh about, and opinions to state. So many ideas and expressing your emotions whittled down to what you can scratch on a boogie board. You pass the time silently contemplating what you can no longer do or relive the "good ole days," as these days in your past seem a world away, unable to fathom that some of these were last year or the year before. You are so much more than what others physically see, so much more to contribute to the world, and so much to express. You are more than the quiet, frail, beautiful woman existing in front of them. There is so much more to your life than what others only see in pictures. They don't know the strength you have exhibited your whole life, your motivation for staying around with those you love just a little bit longer, or the history of your wisdom and experiences. They will never know the depth of your love for your husband, family, the pride you exhibit for your children and grandchildren.

What I am left with is this. You are still here, you are still Mom. Every breath signals hope, every smile illuminates your light, and every touch evokes emotion. Your muted laugh still fills the room, and your eyes dance with joy. Those in the room still fight to be seated next to you to enjoy their time spent in your presence. The reflection I see when I am with you is love, determination, and so much beauty and joy. I see a larger-than-life human that I cannot begin to explain my honor in calling her Mom. You may think you're silent, but your actions speak the loudest in the room; your inspiration has no bounds, you exude infinite love, and the courage you inspire can supply an army. You approach each day with a resolve one cannot measure, a willingness to make the day count, and a gratefulness for each of your blessings. You are awe-inspiring, amazing, and so loved – a day in the life with you is one I will never take for granted.

CHAPTER FIFTEEN

Life Lessons

—

Mom's 80th birthday was approaching in a few weeks, so we turned our attention to making her celebration everything it could be, as she had commented early into the diagnosis that she wanted to make it to her 80th, so as not to say she died in her 70s. She said it sounded better! With pandemic guidelines in place, we each made a plan to isolate at home prior to our gathering. We solicited photos and birthday wishes using videos from family and friends who could not attend our celebration, and my older brother compiled a video, complete with music and birthday "reels," to showcase her life with all of us. We made banners, ordered an ice cream cake— one of the foods we thought she could handle—and planned our party. Not the 80th birthday celebration that I had always envisioned for her, but we persevered and embraced every ounce of those preparations, despite our heartbreaking reality. And so we planned how to make this special and inclusive of family, despite the pandemic and concerns associated with it. As we prepared to celebrate her beautiful life, I continued to write.

February 11, 2021

What is the most important lesson you learned in school? It's interesting to me that we can navigate through elementary school, high school, and even college, and yet still be unprepared for life upon graduation. We spend years attending, getting up each day, being present, focusing on the lessons, and preparing for the ultimate quiz or test to showcase our knowledge. Reflecting on those years for me, I discovered how many instances when I struggled with the material, hesitant to ask the questions, and wondered why we spent the time covering chapters that seemed meaningless. But through it all, I persevered, accentuated my strengths, and eventually acquired enough of the lesson to make sense of the course.

Ironically, I sit here faced with yet another course, only this time the course is unmanageable, difficult, and I am left feeling unprepared and unorganized. How do I begin to comprehend the material when I am unsure of the course description, a blank syllabus, and no seasoned professor? Strangely, this class is not paid for financially; it is a gift uniquely given to each of us to complete. I keep trying to learn the material, focus on key elements of the chapters, underlining in my head the important points, but none of it fits; I am unable to understand the goal of this course. And then it dawns on me, the objective of the class is wisdom. No textbooks exist, and we are left to be challenged on our own. And prerequisites include utilizing moments and past lessons in our lives to finish this class.

The course is titled "Life," and through this course, we learn to accept challenges, new opportunities, and "making lemonade when life hands you lemons," even though it may be bitter and not what you ordered. What can I say that I've learned from this course? I have learned that even though the lesson is difficult and nothing in it makes sense, you forge ahead and determine your outcome. There are still chapters that I can't wrap my head around, but just like my earlier years, I keep at it and search for what steps I am leaving out of the equation. I ask questions when appropriate to help me grasp the answers, I eliminate unnecessary challenges that do not lead to hope, and most importantly, I do not give up in my pursuit of passing the class. Sometimes I prefer to skip a chapter, but I vow to always be present in the moment, for there are lessons and opportunities to be gained by stumbling through it. I may not always enjoy the material, but I have discovered that the infinite requirement needed for this course is love. The objective now seems so clear to me; what a waste of instruction it would have been not to attempt the course itself.

CHAPTER SIXTEEN

Honoring the Dash

—

What a fabulous 80th birthday celebration we had with her. I recall watching her smile, beaming with pride, watching all the activities flourish around the condo room where she was permanently seated. The St. Patrick decorations, although difficult to find through the moving boxes, were displayed around the room, along with many balloons, streamers, and birthday signs. She was able to wear her usual birthday shirt, a shamrock sweatshirt, complete with a flashing shamrock light necklace purchased for the celebration! She wore her shamrock earrings and socks, reminiscent and reflective of years of birthday celebrations on St. Patrick's Day. She feverishly wrote on her boogie board how thankful and blessed she was to have all of us there and for organizing such a wonderful party. As family members arrived, her grandchildren fought for space near her, eager to be close to her. What she couldn't understand was our aching desire to make this as perfect as she was. Our goal was to fill the space with all of the love she had put out into the world. My brothers and I each found moments to sit by her, and I witnessed the exchanges she had with them. Her silent laugh echoed loudly in my heart. She had a way of always making us feel seen, heard, and loved, even in the smallest of ways. With her boogie board as her guide, she wrote her appreciation within the moments of these interactions. My brothers could always make her laugh, and they continued their part, with her recognition caught in her written response. Watching her delight with my older brother, she quickly scribbled, "makes me laugh for all these years." When my younger brother stole time with her a little while later, her written response was captured with "a very special son." My brothers and I had always teased each other about who was the favorite child. What siblings don't do this? And so we had to laugh when, later that day, she wrote, "Jenn has moved up to #1 child," her witty sense of humor fueling the moment. She always found ways to distinguish her pride in us, complementing our individualities. Her sisters were with us, and we all enjoyed the laughter and memories. But catching glimpses of her in her chair that day, I kept recalling the statement she had made months prior, "I miss my life." And as I sat there on this beautiful day, watching her, memories flooded my head, bringing back birthdays from years past, picnics, graduations, and Christmases spent together. All of the traditions that went along with these gatherings had a common thread: she filled our lives with a contagious laugh, shared funny stories, encouraged the pursuit of promises and dreams, and exuded pride in her family, always believing in the best.

I remember watching her as she looked around the room, as if surveying all the blessings in her life, all present in one room. I reminisce about that day a lot, as I like to remember the joy of her smile and the twinkle in her eyes.

Two weeks later, Gene called and said that she wasn't feeling well, experiencing some pain, and maybe I should not bring my kids this time for our routine visit. However, our middle son chose to come, as he really wanted to spend time with her. I told our other two children that we would see her again on Easter, which was in a few days. I was anticipating the visit, as I had recently received both doses of my COVID-19 vaccine and had waited the two-week timeframe, and I was excited to visit without a mask. Based on the information we had received and my isolation, I could feel safe visiting without a mask, a desire of hers since the pandemic began.

We drove up and visited, and played our usual game of Farkle with her and her sister. She was weaker that day, quietly sitting, but still smiling. She struggled with using the Sara Stedy, her body weaker than before, and she seemed unsure of her current ability to navigate the transportation device. Was she anxious? Scared? I also spent some time getting her registered in the ALS Registry Database on the computer. The registry consisted of questions about her current residence, background, and veteran status, among others.

We left that day, saying our normal goodbyes, snow covering the ground on that April Fool's Day. Easter was arriving in three days, and she was looking forward to it, one of her favorite holidays. After we got in the car, Gene ran outside, and I was summoned back inside. She had a few other things to tell me, and for whatever reason, I don't remember what they were. I do remember, though, coming back in to see her smiling face with her boogie board on her lap. I remember laughing with her as she commented on my winter coat looking dirty. I replied that it was in the laundry pile, but I needed to wear it to see her before I could wash it and put it away until next winter. After all, who could have predicted it would snow on April Fool's Day? And then she wrote on her board "Hoppy Easter," and I smiled and said, "Well, don't worry, we will be back in a few days for Easter, and we can celebrate together." I recall the drive home that night, and on our drive, I called my brothers and told them to come soon, as I sensed what was coming.

We arrived home, and I continued to think about the day's visit with her. She struggled to keep her head upright when using the Sara Steady and seemed so much weaker than I had witnessed the other day. I remember contemplating what I could bring for Easter and what to put in her basket for our next visit.

The phone rang 30 minutes after we arrived home, and it was Gene, asking to speak to my husband. And then I saw the look on his face and heard him say, "Oh, God, I am so sorry," and for a brief moment, I thought maybe it was another trip to the hospital. But I sensed this was different, and then my husband gently told me that she had passed.

I heard someone screaming and grabbed a pillow to stifle the screams, beating the cushions of the couch in disbelief and anger. The screaming continued, and it wasn't until I noticed I was out of breath that I realized the person screaming was myself. It was as if I had run several miles, as my beating of the pillow, screaming, and the enormity of the news had broken me and taken all of my energy with it in that one moment. My mind raced. This can't be right, and all I could say was "no, no, no, no" on repeat.

I am not sure how long I had been in this position on the couch, but I finally looked up and realized this was not a dream. My husband handed me the phone, and I spoke with Gene. The exasperation in his voice erased any doubt in my mind that this was the new reality that I had to come to terms with somehow. I told him I would contact my brothers and that he could talk with the coroner, the funeral home, and my mom's older sister, who lived nearby.

This is the call that I had dreaded since I was a kid after losing our dad, and now she was gone. My world and heart were shattered with two words, "she's gone."

I contacted my brothers, in birth order as I always did, and shared the heartbreaking news. After my phone calls, I began to reflect on a time when my senses were so alive with promise as a five-year-old, and now completely shattered and muted, much like her voice, with this life-changing news. I cannot feel her hand in mine again, I cannot hear that joyful laugh or encouraging voice, I cannot see her beautiful face light up when one of us enters the room, I cannot smell her perfume or baked goods fill the air, and I cannot taste her delicious banana bread or chocolate chip cookies. Instead, I feel my heart breaking into a million pieces, I hear the screams of my own pain echoed in my brothers reactions when I call them to share this news, I see my tears and those of my husband and children, a constant flow, reflected in the mirror, I smell the pillow where I laid my head to muffle my own screams at the news, and I have a taste for nothing but anger with our loss. I wrote this last letter shortly after she passed.

April 7, 2021

The warm sun hits my face, spring has sprung, and the crocuses are beginning their outward stretch towards the sky. Your favorite time of year has begun, a time for rebirth, to welcome the sweet smell of fresh air, listen to the birds' chirping, and announce their plans for nesting. So many new beginnings, brought back to life after a dark, cold winter season. I marvel at how the bulbs find their way to the surface of the soil, awaiting their moment to shine and be majestic, if only for a few months of the year. But year after year, this is the ritual that encompasses this season. We patiently wait and anticipate this time of year as it serves as a welcome to the warm, sunny days ahead, when outdoor life awakens after the dormancy of winter. I like to think that I enjoy this awakening as much as you do, as it signals hope for the upcoming months of the year.

Only this year, my spring feels a bit more muted and cloudier than in years past. The emerging flowers still offer hope and inspiration, which I find play a vital role in my approach to my own life. I am amazed that the bulbs, although buried under the soil, strive to reach the surface, as if on cue, and maintain their annual routine. What happens when those bulbs are deprived of a link to survival and unable to participate in the rebirth? I noticed this one day in our garden, the normally sweet-smelling hyacinths were covered with a bucket, not receiving sunshine, water, warm air, all signals to release their potential. And yet, after removing the bucket, to my surprise, the stems had broken through the soil, weakened, but there. And that's where the beauty of God's grace steps in, carefully ensuring that each bulb serves its purpose. Much like our own lives, when a "bucket" covers our growth, we still strive for purpose, weakened but existing. When we open ourselves up to hope, the "bucket" comes off, and we can flourish in the light and warmth so we can reach our fullest potential.

But this year, spring signaled the time in our lives when you passed away, the moment when time seemed to stand still for me. How are we left here with the beautiful flowers, some of your favorites, and not with you to enjoy their beauty, fragrance, and purpose? What happened to our ritual of nature's rebirth with you? Although you were weakened, you still had purpose, you still had potential – I still had hope and fought with every ounce of my being that you would be here "just a little longer." But reflecting on our last few days together, I realize that you still had broken through the barriers of your world, fighting to stay with us for just a little longer, but your body had weakened. And then God's grace showed me your rebirth, not with us, but with Him. Your purpose, although seemingly limited in time, was served with us, and it was now time for you to rest. You had reached your potential, fulfilling a life full of love, joy, thankfulness, and motherhood. So, when I witness the bulbs emerge every spring and the sweet smell of the hyacinths reach my nose, nature's rebirth begins to unfold, and I will always think of you!!

What I Know Now

—

What a beautiful life. How could such an amazing life be taken with such a cruel and unrelenting disease? First and foremost, what I learned from watching my mom face this disease is to always be present in life's moments, live with passion and empathy, and engage with those around you. Take the time to appreciate laughable moments, the comfort of long hugs, and count your blessings. I cannot state this without surmising how incredibly blessed we all are for knowing and loving her, as we all felt the impact of her legacy. She taught us that, despite the circumstances, to continue to persevere, focus on life and the people in front of you, and have the wisdom and courage to accept the challenge.

My memories of my life with her can never be replaced, and I think she knew this as she entered her final months. She never once complained about her situation, nor changed her can-do attitude, especially with those close to her. It was as if she believed, as I did, that she could "beat the odds" of this disease, and she continued her fight until the very end. She complied with her physical therapist, obliged us while we entered her information into the ALS Registry, and continued entertaining us with her prowess at the game of Farkle. She did not quit, which in itself is the larger lesson in all of this. Instead, she remained determined to stay with us until her body chose to quit. I cannot think of a better lesson to live my life by than to always spread joy, even without making a sound, and be grateful for the years you have and with whom you spend them. It was a mere five months after her official diagnosis before she passed away—a lifetime of memories, lessons, joy, laughter, and love culminated in those 157 days.

I hope that by reading this book, you will gain a glimpse into our journey with ALS. I have learned that behind every person is a story, and we will never know its full extent until we pause to understand it. We can all learn from each other, and each of us can apply this knowledge when we encounter another person facing difficulties.

Always trying to process my grief, I took up writing again a few months after losing her. I thought it would be therapeutic, and, in a way, it was. It was honest, brutal, angry, sad, inconsolable, and yet, hopeful. There are many stages of grief, and there is no time limit, as I continue to be reminded. I took my time to adjust and process, then began my crusade to help others facing this cruel and unrelenting journey.

July 13, 2021

I am different today. I have been for several months now. I don't laugh the same, breathe the same, think the same. It is difficult to think that this change is now a part of who I am, as I will never be the same person I was before you passed. Waves of emotions overcome me some days. I write down my feelings in an effort to release what I am feeling, but I am still left with "I wanted more time with you."

I have been reading about how grief affects us all differently, and I think that's what resonates the most with me: we all process a loss uniquely. I keep telling myself to embrace the enjoyable moments with you, so many! I revert to conversations or moments and wonder, "What would you do, what would you say?" You made me who I am today; your belief in me gave me my strength, and your fun sense of humor allowed me to see the brighter side of things. Even writing this now, I am finding that there are no words that I can use to shine a light on just how beautiful and loving you were to all of us. I keep writing in the hopes that I will find some solace in written words. I will, one day, find myself smiling more with memories of you. When I reach for the phone to call you, I will instead vocalize my thoughts out loud to you. When I go to bed at night, I look at your picture and tell you I love you and that I miss you, but one day, I will smile when I lay my head on my pillow, and my dreams will be full of vivid, wonderful memories of you. I can sometimes feel your presence in my dreams, as if you are still watching over me like you did when I was a child, ensuring all was safe. Your love for me made me a better person, and I am so grateful for that. I knew as I got older, our time would be limited together, but I didn't expect, in a million years, that it would be this short. I will always need you; I will always miss you, and I will never be the same without you. But you showed me courage, that love has no bounds, and sometimes our strength comes from within you when you didn't even know it existed. There is no time limit on grief; no one grieves the same way, but we all have a way of processing it in order to begin this "different" life.

I try to keep on writing, as you always encouraged me to do. I took a break because I lost my muse, you, but I will continue, as you showed me to never give up on your passions. After all, it is one of my ways to process your passing. I still find funny moments in my day when I think of how you would react to that moment, how you would laugh at the silliness of it all, right along with me. I miss sharing my triumphs, the kids' accomplishments, and my sometimes mundane routine. I miss our special times, such as watching you put on your makeup while we talked, helping you style your hair, and you asking me if your outfit looks presentable. As I sort through your clothes, all that I am left with is the thought of "I don't want the clothes, I want you." I miss your smell, as each time I inhale and smell the faintest of your perfume brings comfort. I smile when I reflect on you wearing our matching sweater, washing your face before bed, greeting us at your front door, or sitting with us at the end of the day. Your voice still echoes in my mind, your laugh, your excitement when hearing good news, and your compassion when needed. I am so grateful for having those memories, but what I wouldn't give to hear that sweet sound in my ears again. My eyes sting some days, needing more laughter and less crying. How is it that you're no longer physically here with us? Still so unfathomable. And I know others have gone through this process, especially you when losing Dad. I know it's different when losing a spouse, but the pain of losing you is all that I can compare this to in my life. I remember losing Dad, I remember how much you were affected and transformed by this. But you showed sheer grace and strength in the face of such a horrific tragedy that I learned from you how to be strong, accept the challenges that life brings, and endure and embrace your changed self. This is what I rely on now in this moment when missing you. When we lost Dad, it was sudden, ripped away from us in a swift moment in time. In fact, due to my young age, I didn't process the loss immediately; it took some time for me to realize the severity, the finality, of it all. And with you, the finality of it all, the severity, was all I could think of, knowing and comprehending what it all meant. I don't know which is easier.

I see the flowers in my garden that I planted especially for you begin to bloom, the cardinals appearing suddenly surrounding your garden, and find some peace in knowing you are still with me, trying so hard to send me a sign that you're with me. I see you, feel you, during moments of my day. I know you are with me when I hear laughter, reliving our memories with you, witnessing joy with your grandchildren, and relishing in our blessings. I thank God for you. I know there is a reason that He called you home when He did, and there is no bargaining with that, although I would love that opportunity! One day, far from now, I will understand, but for now, I am left with a hole in my heart that I know will never be filled, but oh so grateful that you once filled it!!

ALWAYS LEAVE SMILING

Her laugh is what resonates in my day, and sometimes I catch myself playing a video I recorded years before her diagnosis, when her hearty, contagious laughter filled the room. I am reminded that in that sound were years of perseverance, resilience, and courage, that enabled her to love her life, be thoroughly engaged in the lessons, and thrive. She left others always wanting more of her and her inspiration. I never took that for granted, and for that lesson, I am forever grateful.

RESOURCES

Advocate and become someone's voice, participate, and be present. I began the month after her passing by speaking to Congress and other legislators about improving access to ALS drugs, such as AMX0035. With COVID-19, focus was on creating a vaccine and obtaining FDA approval, so the pursuit of obtaining FDA approval for AMX0035 fell to the sidelines. Write to your congressional representatives and contact news organizations and magazines to share your story about ALS. This disease needs more understanding and funding than is currently allotted.

Register for ALS Walks - create a team and raise funds to help the ALS organizations in their research, equipment loans, care giving support, and more. Or, simply make a donation to the organization.

Surround yourself with those you love, remember to laugh, hug tightly, embrace everyone's differences, and make room for personal growth. Learn patience, humility, and be generous with your time. Express gratitude to each life you encounter, greet new obstacles and adventures with optimism, and be aware of the lesson.

Enroll in the Centers for Disease Control National ALS Registry. Monitored and maintained by the CDC, this registry collects and stores data for ALS patients, including background details, the US location of the ALS patient, environmental exposures, and other relevant information. It is used to try to track clusters of ALS cases, causes, and more to help pinpoint direct links to disease development and determine a cause for this cruel disease. Take the time to enroll; it is currently voluntary, but crucial in determining the underlying cause of this disease!

Contact CMS (Centers for Medicare & Medicaid Services) and urge them to recognize the rights and needs of ALS patients. In April of 2021, CMS finally granted allowance for ALS patients to use Telehealth as a viable means of communicating with doctors. More work is needed for ALS patients and their families. CMS needs to realign its priorities in helping those with ALS, such as allowing the ALS specialists to dictate what is needed, not CMS, in terms of care for these patients. Patients need access to OT, PT, and Speech therapy to maintain muscle and joint function, keep them limber, and assist with speech. During my mom's battle, this was not allotted, despite the objections from her ALS specialists. Home health care services need to be considered part of the coverage, as many families are using GoFundMe accounts and other avenues to fund this costly but much-needed option.

Create a sign-up for those asking what they can do to help. For example, I created a sign-up for help with meals (carefully considering those with ALS who have food restrictions), visits (to provide a break for caregivers), or greeting cards (to mail to maintain their spirits). Create a social media page to share with your ALS loved one, for those who are unable to visit in person. They can share photographs, memories, and more.

Record videos, take photographs, ELICIT conversations, and ask questions about their lives, as vivid memories reside within what may appear to be a silent observer. Do something spontaneous with them or for them, as there are memories to be made spending time in their presence.

Contact your local state ombudsman to help advocate for care for those in nursing homes or long-term care facilities when you have issues or concerns that cannot be resolved. I contacted the local ombudsman to assist my mom during her nursing home stay.

ORGANIZATIONS

NIH (National Institutes of Health) for rare diseases, where you can discover and research clinical research and current trials.

Local ALS Chapters - an invaluable organization in helping those navigate this cruel disease. Not only do they offer support, but also educational classes, virtual meetings with other ALS patients and caregivers, a loan closet for life-sustaining equipment at home and in nursing homes, and grants for caregivers and their families to lessen the burden of the cost of care.

ALS Association - a trove of information dedicated to finding a cure for ALS. Information includes understanding ALS, navigating ALS for patients and caregivers, research, and advocacy.

pALS - an organization run by the ALS Association to help persons with **ALS**. Information includes funds that can help families obtain equipment and other resources.

Mobility Works - a van rental company in Ohio, where caregivers can rent wheelchair accessible vans for transportation for ALS patients. This was beneficial for us; it provides an opportunity to get ALS patients outside for a "joy ride" or to a doctor's appointment.

Team Gleason Foundation- an organization created by Steve Gleason and his family to help others with ALS. They provide speaking devices, grants, and support for pALS and their families.

ALS Blogs - I found these blogs helpful in determining my approach to care giving and also sharing information about ALS. They also provided some insight into what others have gone through, what was helpful, and suggestions for others.

Catfish Foundation - created in honor of Jim "Catfish" Hunter, grants and information to help offset the costs of those living with ALS and their families. Those running this organization are not only helpful and supportive, but were extremely kind and empathetic, just when I needed them.

Items to consider when living with ALS at home:

Bold indicates item might be obtained through the ALS Loan Closet

Hospital bed, electric

Boogie Board writing tablet- pALS can use this to communicate

Chux pads - used for bed, if needed

Sara Stedy - for transferring patients from one area to another in the home.

In-Home Health Care Aides - inquire about training of aides, schedules, access to a 24-hour call center, policies on aide coverage, aide background working with ALS patients, duties covered when the ALS patient is resting, etc.

Tankless oxygen tanks, if needed

Adjustable Arm Table/Monitor holder - allows ALS patients to access a computer or a Tobii device without using their arm strength

Invest in a comfortable, padded mattress pad for the hospital bed

Adjustable bedside table with wheels

Bedpan

Bedside commode

Shower chair

Bi-Pap machine

Ice machine - crushed ice to aid in thirst, if needed

Voice banking machine - Tobii device, iPad, or eye gaze equipment for speech

Lift chair or **Broda chair recliner**

Laptrays - helpful when pALS using speaking devices or a computer, release the heaviness on their laps

Wheelchair - motorized or manual wheelchair

Things to take note of when declaring hospice:

Hospice is in place to provide care for those with a terminal disease. Palliative care is geared to improving one's quality of life. Hospice provides STNAs (state-tested nursing assistants) to assess medical needs and aides to help with personal care, 24-hour on-call nursing or doctor needs, massage therapy, equipment, and a range of other services, all 100% covered by Medicare. Additionally, hospice offers chaplains and a social worker. Things that are **NOT** covered include medications to improve quality of life, PT, OT, or speech therapy.

My first speech to Congress on the ALS Advocacy Day
at Capitol Hill, June 14, 2021:

HOW DOES ALS AFFECT MY LIFE?

My mom was diagnosed with advanced-stage sporadic ALS last November. She passed away approximately five months after receiving her diagnosis. I would like to begin by thanking our local ALS chapter for their support and guidance in helping us navigate her fight against ALS.

What began over a year ago was her quest to find answers to her "floppy foot," which was the initial symptom. With no family history of the disease, she spent over a year going to doctor appointments, actively searching for answers. She was determined to get her life back, visiting her PCP multiple times and seeking answers from several neurologists. She was told it was due to a nerve compression in her spine and untreated scoliosis, was scheduled for surgery, and she was hopeful. She endured the surgery and subsequent rehab isolated from her family, but unbeknownst to her, she was entering a battle for which she was not given the ammunition. We need to do better. ALS patients deserve better.

Due to her diagnosis with advanced-stage ALS, she was unable to participate in clinical trials. Providing more funding to create more opportunities for clinical trials, including trials for all stages of ALS, is essential. My mom would have participated in any type of trials that might stop or slow the progression of her condition, anything that could provide some kind of hope for her.

My mom, like most ALS patients, had been healthy her whole life, and she faced the news of her ALS diagnosis courageously. She fought to the best of her ability, at 79 years of age, against this brutal disease, but also had to contend with the denial of services by Medicare that were so needed, such as PT, OT, speech, and respiratory therapy. CMS determined that she would not benefit from these services, although fiercely advocated by ALS specialists. She deserved every tool available to fight this disease and to be given the appropriate equipment in her arsenal. She was so much more than her member ID. Her mind remained unchanged during all of this as she gave witness to what ALS was doing to her body. She was unable to talk, hug her family, cry, or even scream over the frustration of it all. There is nothing more heartbreaking.

Our family was also faced with the costs of providing 24-hour care to meet the needs of her rapidly declining health. I applied for grants and assistance where I could, but the financial costs, even with her long-term care insurance, could not keep up with the overwhelming burden. The cost of bringing in aides to help with her care in her last few months was $35,000. For many families, covering these types of medically necessary costs is problematic, as these are unforeseeable circumstances that are difficult to plan for in retirement or at any point during one's lifetime.

I also feel that ALS needs to be recognized as a reportable disease. This disease, which has been around for more than 80 years, can strike anyone at any time. Case counts fluctuate, and more funding to help the ALS Registry house this information in a central database will help with research as to possible causes or links to triggers of this disease.

How does ALS affect my life? It took away an irreplaceable part of my light, laughter, joy, and a piece of my heart. Her case can never be an example of what others should go through. We have the doctors, the services, and the specialists available to make ALS a livable disease by 2030. What we are missing is funding for research, awareness, educating, and training for

PCPs, treatments, and insurance benefits to aid those in their battle. My mom was not given a fair fight; she had more to contribute, more love to share, and more people to inspire. Please use our story so that no other family has to endure what we did, helplessly watching a loved one succumb to this cruel disease, especially in a matter of months. I, personally, will do whatever it takes, as her fight is now my fight. ALS might have won in her battle, but I am now her voice, and I will fiercely advocate and continue the fight against this disease for her and others.

Thank you for your time and for providing me with the opportunity to speak with you today.

My second speech to Congress on the ALS Advocacy Day
at Capitol Hill, June 21, 2022:[1]

I would like to thank you for the opportunity to speak with you and explain to you my personal connection to ALS and why this opportunity is important to me. I am able to use my voice for those who cannot speak, as in the case of my mom. She was diagnosed with ALS at 79 years of healthy living. Like many of those diagnosed with ALS, they are healthy, vibrant, and the light in their loved one's eyes. I would like to provide you with a brief background to my mom's story and why I am here today. She spent over a year searching for answers from multiple doctors to determine the cause of her now explained symptoms, a "drop foot," and sometimes finding it difficult to whistle and swallow. But these symptoms were random, not consistent, and some days showed improvement. When she was finally officially diagnosed with ALS in the late fall of 2020, the country was still in the throes of the pandemic, and she was recovering from back surgery, as this was one of the many procedures she had been advised to undergo to address her symptoms. As we know now, she was misdiagnosed for over a year. What a vital waste of time in order to participate in Riluzole or Radicava, or clinical trials. It was too late at that point, as she was diagnosed with sporadic, advanced-stage ALS. Every person deserves the right to prepare for the fight of their lives. Due to her advanced stage of the disease, she was eliminated from participation in clinical trials, which I had been researching. She was determined to keep fighting, and I recall her once telling me that she "missed her life." I was provided with some hope when I read about AMX0035 in ALS blogs and research guides. Patients who used it were hopeful and felt their symptoms reach a stalemate or even improve. I recall contacting her ALS specialist and asking

---

1 When this letter was written in 2022, AMX0035 was a promising new clinical trial that offered some hope to ALS patients. While this is no longer a treatment option, the pursuit and importance remain the same: to offer hope for ALS patients.

if my mom could at least qualify for TUDCA, only to be told that it would be effective unless it was used in combination with sodium phenylbutrate. What is most surprising to me is that these two drugs are currently approved individually, one as a supplement and one used to treat pediatric urea disorder. AMX0035 may not be the cure, but combined with the only other two treatment medications for ALS, those in the trials in Europe showed a slowing of their functional decline. In fact, an article from ALS News Today from 2021, Sabrina Paganoni, MD, and PhD, is quoted from the annual American Academy of Neurology meeting, saying, "AMX0035 is the first to show a combination of both functional and survival benefits for people living with ALS." What wonderful news for those able to qualify for a clinical trial and not receive the placebo. How can the FDA refute these findings from a specialist in the field, stating that there is not enough evidence to approve the benefit of AMX0035? How can they determine the benefit when they are not fighting for their lives? My mom, like many other patients, would have done anything to have more time with her family, to experience hope in the face of insurmountable, grim obstacles. Can you honestly imagine what it must be like to remain unchanged in your opinion or emotions but lose the ability to speak or share your thoughts with others? Having others, such as caregivers or home health aides, dictate your daily routine while you are still of sound mind? She urgently and courageously wanted to express her thoughts and lost her ability to speak, but her desire to do whatever it took to remain with us never faltered. Unfortunately, she lost her battle a mere 5 months after her official diagnosis, but during that time, the FDA granted emergency approval for COVID-19 vaccines to prevent hospitalizations and deaths from COVID-19. What a shame the same cannot be given for AMX0035, to provide hope and possible benefits to those living with ALS. The need is urgent; ALS patients can't wait. There is no time. I remember telling my mom that AMX0035 is coming, it is promising, and

I am not giving up on her. I was hopeful, even after she passed, that this could prevent other families from going through what we did in such a short, pandemic-filled time with her. She could not wait, and neither can others. If they cannot speak, we will. If they could express their desires, why take away that right from them by denying them to make a judgment on whether they want to use AMX0035 in their arsenal? I am only asking that we explain to the FDA that more trials take time, time ALS patients don't have. Based on research, the two drugs that make up AMX0035 are not harmful; in fact, they have both been approved previously. Why delay providing hope?

I will never be the same without her, but I am blessed BECAUSE of her. I wish you could have known her, as she was the epitome of what we all hope to accomplish in life. Her laughter and her light filled every room she entered. Her battle was unforgiving and relentless, but her life mattered, and her love endures. Please consider this request from the FDA in the approval of AMX0035, as so many more loved ones' lives are at stake.

ABOUT THE AUTHOR

Jennifer Bernay has enjoyed being an educator for over 14 years, beginning as a Pre-K teacher and currently teaching third grade. Outside of school, she enjoys spending time with family and friends, going for walks, writing, and working in her garden. She enjoys watching her favorite sports teams from Cleveland, Ohio, and her alma mater, The Ohio State University Buckeyes. She grew up in Stow, OH, before moving to Columbus, where she resides with her husband and their three children. They embrace time spent with their children and often travel to visit them at their respective colleges, all located in Ohio.

In her spare time, she focuses on finding joy in the everyday experiences and continuing the lessons she learned from her mother. She also enjoys family trips to Lake Erie in the summer to relax and unwind.

Jennifer continues to raise awareness for ALS patients and caregivers, and provides others with advice based on her experience with her mother's diagnosis. She can be reached at authorjennifer.bernay@gmail.com for media appearances to share her experience with ALS awareness, grief, and hope.